DATE DUE

DE 1 '98			

DEMCO 38-296

The Future of Europe

The Future of Europe

Peter Coffey
US WEST Chair
University of St. Thomas
Minneapolis, USA

Edward Elgar

JN 15 .C54 1995

Coffey, Peter.

The future of Europe

Aldershot
Hants GU11 3HR
England

Edward Elgar Publishing Company
Old Post Road
Brookfield
Vermont 05036
USA

British Library Cataloguing in Publication Data
Coffey, Peter
  Future of Europe
  I. Title
  330.94

Library of Congress Cataloguing in Publication Data
Coffey, Peter
    The Future of Europe / Peter Coffey
p. cm.
    1. European federation   2. Treaty on European Union (1992)
    3. European Economic Community 4. Europe – Politics and Government –
      1989
    I. Title
    JN15.C54
    321' .04' 1994—dc20   93-49829 CIP

ISBN 1 85278 586 1
     1 85278 587 X (paperback)

Printed in Great Britain at the University Press, Cambridge

Contents

Figures and Tables

Acknowledgements

Although the opinions expressed in this book are entirely my own, I am nevertheless deeply grateful to a number of friends and colleagues who have, over the past months, agreed to discuss issues of major current importance with me. In particular, I wish to thank Richard Blackhurst of the GATT Secretariat, Pierre-André Buigues of the European Commission, Monica Den Boer of Edinburgh University, Robert Farlow of the University of St. Thomas, Andrew Hughes-Hallet of the Universities of Princeton and Strathclyde, Alexis Jacquemin of the European Commission and the University of Louvain-La-Neuve, André Louw of the European Commission, Michael Metcalf of the University of Minnesota, Livio-Amedeo Missir of the European Commission, Andrew Scott of the Europa Instituut at Edinburgh University and Alan Sked of the London School of Economics.

Special thanks are due to the editors of Agence Europe, Brussels, who have kindly allowed me to reproduce the appendices at the end of this book which originally appeared in *Europe*.

Last, but by no means least, I am grateful to my assistant, Patrick Dykhoff, who has transcribed the manuscript and prepared the index for this book.

Introduction

When I first set out to write this book, my initial proposal for the title was 'Europe à la Carte'. With the benefit of hindsight, my first proposal would have been much more appropriate than the present more elegant one, *The Future of Europe*. Although my original title would not have pleased some of my distinguished friends in the Commission of the European Communities in Brussels, I believe that it not only describes the Europe we know today but also the Europe which we shall live with in the immediate future. Our Europe with its wonderful and irritating national differences could not, in the immediate future, become a United States of Europe because we cherish our national differences too much. In contrast, the early European settlers in America wanted to get away from Europe and consequently created the United States – *voilà la différence!*

Although I myself have always desired a great degree of European integration, I do not want it at any price since this could destroy us all. Also, I feel that many of our national differences do make us richer. Consequently, our main concern, especially after all the civil wars we have fought in Europe over the centuries, should be to safeguard and cherish basic human rights. I shall return to this theme several times in this book.

I have been accused by my friends of being an incurable optimist. However, it must be said that Europe has made fabulous progress since the end of World War II. For example, the creation of the European Coal and Steel Community and the signing, in 1963, of the Treaty of Co-operation between France and the Federal German Republic have made war between the two countries unthinkable – at least in the immediate future. Then, despite the current recession, the present

1

wealth of Western Europe bears no comparison with the ruins, poverty and lack of energy of 1945. More recently, the collapse of Communism has opened up undreamed of possibilities – economic, political and social in nature – for the formerly separated parts of the continent. At this point, the major question we are facing is whether we are capable of grasping these fabulous and historically unique opportunities which have been offered to us. Unfortunately, I fear that our leaders are too mesmerized by their immediate short-term interests and could, alas, miss this crucially important bus of history.

WHICH EUROPE?

Just as the United States is not the Americas, so the European Community is not Europe. In both cases, however, they are the economic and political locomotives of their continents, and neighbouring countries want to be closely linked and even to be integrated with them.

In the specific case of the European Community, we find ourselves faced with the dilemma of deepening and/or widening the Community. Here, as with so many other choices, the solution would seem to be one of adopting a policy of 'Europe à la carte'.

Whatever our preferences may be, we find ourselves at a crossroads where we must take decisions in a number of important policy areas – it is, in fact, the imperative necessity of taking these decisions that influenced the structure of this work and which has necessitated a careful selecting of policy areas to be examined. But the basic question which I shall try to answer by the end of this work is, 'What kind of Europe do we want?' Personally speaking, after the enormous human sacrifices we made during World War II, I certainly want a democratic Europe without racism and other incomprehensible horrors (has no one learned anything from history?) where all citizens enjoy the same basic rights, as so eloquently laid down in the European Convention on Human Rights. I shall also return to this theme on many occasions in the course of writing this book. However, I am aware that we have to find workable solutions to our current problems and it is the combination of problems and solutions which has influenced the structure of this work.

THE ORGANIZATION OF THE BOOK

At the outset I must admit to having resisted the temptation of including a chapter on the Common (or Crazy?) Agricultural Policy (CAP) of the European Community about which so much has been written in other works. However, I do stress my belief that this CAP is a scandalous misallocation of public resources which bedevils the Community's relations with all countries except Thailand. Instead, following a brief examination and my own interpretation of the historical evolution of European integration since the end of World War II, I decided to examine selected major topical issues and to make, where possible, proposals for policy changes.

Earlier Attempts at Political Union: Common Foreign and Security Policies

The Treaty on European Union does have, among other aims, a major dual objective – the adoption of common foreign and defence policies (possibly leading to common defence). To some observers this goal comes as something of a novelty. It should be remembered, however, that there had been serious attempts among the six EEC Founder Member States, in the early 1960s, to create these common policies. A famous Fouchet Committee was created, but, when President de Gaulle realized the supranational aims of this committee, its chairman, Christian Fouchet, was dispatched to Algeria as Governor-General. France then replaced the idea of supranationality with the official policy of a 'Europe of the nation states'.

Attempts at Forming an Economic and Monetary Union

Equally, the embodiment in the Treaty on European Union of a rather detailed plan for an economic and monetary union (EMU) could mislead students into thinking that this is another EC innovation. Nothing could be further from the truth. The original decision to embark upon the very difficult road leading to a full EMU was taken by the EEC Heads of State and Government in the Hague as early as the end of 1969. Subsequently, the second and definitive Werner Plan of October 1972 became the blueprint for the Community's first attempts at creating an EMU. These took the practical form of the 'Snake in the Tunnel' and the 'Snake Arrangement' which were replaced by the present European Monetary System (EMS) in March 1979. All of these attempts may be interpreted as being a much prolonged intermediate phase of an EMU.

The Record of the Single European Market

So much has already been written and said about the Single European Market (SEM) and the magic of 1992 that many readers will probably believe that little more remains to be said. My aim is therefore not to repeat everything that has already been told, but rather to place the SEM in its historical context as being the logical creation of a real common market as set down in the Treaty of Rome. Also, I believe it important to highlight the possible benefits of reaching all the goals of the SEM in the late 1990s or early twenty-first century and of opening up, for example, the national telecommunications and energy markets.

Equally, it should be noted that the present trend of achieving common standards through the mutual recognition of the national standards of EC Member States does not really constitute absolutely common standards. This development, as has been observed by the new president of the CEN (European Committee of Standards), is disquieting.

The Treaty on European Union

Despite being bombarded from all sides with misleading information about this wearisome Treaty on European Union, and in the specific case of Ireland, being subjected to scandalous bribery, arrogant politicians were brought to their senses by the hardy Danes when, in a referendum in June, last year, they rejected the Treaty. Quite simply, the Danes were fed up of being treated like idiots by their political representatives – acting more like political masters.

The Treaty does include a number of important aims which will, over time, change the political complexion of the Community. Thus, the aims of common foreign and defence policies (possibly leading to common defence) and internal (police) co-operation between EC Member States do harbour great potential changes in the lives of Europe's citizens. Whilst only limited progress is likely with the first two aims, there is already so much progress with police matters (both official and unofficial) that I felt concerned enough to write a separate chapter on the Rights of Citizens and similar matters.

Whilst the Treaty does say much about an EMU and the strict criteria which countries must fulfil if they wish to be eligible for the final stage of such a union, much too little is said about the equally important area of fiscal policy.

The Community's Social Charter is, for the most part, included in the Treaty. Whilst I certainly support the idea of worker representation in enterprises – as practised in Germany – I wonder whether, as was feared by Mrs. Thatcher, the Charter does not constitute a subtle move in the direction of creating a European minimum wage. If so, will not this be economically negative for the poorer Community countries and will it not reduce Europe's competitive ability *vis-à-vis* the United States and Japan?

Although the Treaty does give more power to the European Parliament and imposes a greater degree of co-operation between that body and the Council, I fear that we shall get ever more embroiled in constitutional battles and legalistic mumbo jumbo and that Europe's citizens will feel even more removed from the Community's decision-making process than is presently the case. It was for this reason that I decided to examine the institutions of the Community and to make proposals for their reform.

The European Institutions

Unlike many of my fellow Anglo-Saxons, I am not a Commission-basher. Indeed, all my contacts with my erudite friends in that institution have been both enjoyable and educative. No, the problem is that the Commission, with its inadequate number of experts, is placed in an invidious position because, extraordinarily, it initiates legislation. Thus, I have turned to Alan Sked's sound, wise and excellent proposals for institutional reform (though I do not agree with all of them). I do agree with his proposals that the Commission should have an advisory role to the European Council of Ministers which should initiate legislation. I agree that the Parliament should be composed of representatives from the national parliaments of the EC Member States and that there should be an Upper House. In addition, the very self-centred European Court of Justice should be opened up and should be overseen by a European Supreme Court to which (unlike the present European Court of Justice) there should be a right of appeal. Such a transformation is imperative because Community law takes precedence over national legislation. Furthermore, the present situation is unacceptably undemocratic in nature. In anticipation of the prospective enlargement of the Community, I believe that for reasons of practicality the present number of commissioners should be drastically reduced. Lastly, sooner or later we shall want to have a European Constitution defining our basic rights as citizens of EC Member States, and, hopefully, other European countries. Happily, we do not have to search far for such a constitution since the preamble to the European Convention on Human Rights would be an admirable European Constitution.

Whilst examining the institutions, there is another concern of the most immediate importance – and that is the question of weighted majority voting and the right of veto in the Council of Ministers. This question takes on much greater significance as more countries join the European Community. Although I do not forecast a situation similar to the use of the *liberum veto*[1] in the Polish Parliament, which indirectly led to the dissolution of the Polish State by the end of the eighteenth century, the Community's first attempts, for example, at formulating a common foreign policy (in the case of Bosnia) have, due first to the intransigence of the Germans, and then to the blindness of the British and French, been nothing short of catastrophic. This situation has arisen because of the irresponsible use of the right of veto by these Member States. Clearly, if the EC is to have common foreign and defence policies, something must be done about this right of veto.

Otherwise, in these two policy areas the only alternative is a policy of Europe à la carte. Although this would not be to the Community's credit, it would be the only practical solution.

Enlargement and/or Greater Depth?

From the moment the Treaty on European Union was formulated at the end of 1991, I observed that (provided it was ratified, of course) it would become more difficult for other countries – notably those of Eastern Europe – to become members of the Community. I still believe this to be the case since we have now created a Community which is highly integrated and sophisticated in nature. Before returning to this point it is worth listing the criteria which must be fulfilled if a country wishes even to be considered for EC membership. These are:

1. They must be European countries.
2. They must be multi-party parliamentary democracies.
3. They must be market-type economies.
4. They must respect human rights.

Clearly the Member States of the European Free Trade Association (EFTA) meet all these criteria and negotiations between the EC Commission and Austria, Finland, Norway and Sweden are now well under way.

But of course, the real question is whether, as the Danes and British wish it, we should just go on enlarging the Community or whether, as is the preference of France and Germany, we should first deepen our policies. Morally and legally speaking, provided that applicant countries meet the four aforementioned criteria, there can be no valid reason to exclude them. Instead, in advance of any further enlargement, we have to reform the institutions and make them more efficient. Failure to do this could cause the Community to grind to a halt. This would not prevent some Member States from integrating more quickly among themselves – nor would it prevent selective policy co-operation between countries.

Regarding the future Member States and the negotiations for membership – where are we and where will we go from here? Of all the applicants, Austria probably presents the fewest problems. Austria is already well integrated into the EC, possesses a strong currency and has a fairly prosperous economy.

In contrast, the three Scandinavian states, although they are rich countries, do present problems. They have agricultural policies which are more 'special' than the Community's CAP (though Sweden is trying to reform its own agricultural system). Then, they have major regional problems, and, correctly, they will require special aid and policies for their Arctic and sub-Arctic regions. More specifically, Norway wishes to keep control over its territorial fishing rights whilst the Swedish Temperance Organization insists on keeping the Swedish state's horrific monopoly for alcohol.

But, what about other countries? Turkey, as is its right under the protocol of the Treaty of Ankara (which established its association with the EC), requested full Community membership. This request was turned down on the grounds that the time was not yet ripe. But, Turkey cannot wait forever. Despite the fact that it is a lay Muslim state, it is a European country of the greatest strategic importance to the West. Surely, as its economy becomes stronger and its human rights record improves, the time will come when Turkey should be admitted to the Community as a full member.

Also, more recently, such progress has been made in reducing tariffs between the EC and Turkey that it is expected that a customs union will be formed between the two parties by 1995.

And what of the countries of Eastern Europe and the former Soviet Union? What kind of arrangements has the Community made with and what should it do in future for these countries? Because of the importance of this subject, I have devoted a whole chapter to Eastern Europe.

Policies for Eastern Europe

The Commission of the European Community did, with admirable speed, start to respond to the immediate educational and technical needs of the countries of Eastern Europe and the former Soviet Union the moment the Berlin Wall was demolished. These took the form of the TEMPUS Programme which finances projects between educational institutions in the EC and Eastern Europe. The PHARE Programme (which groups 24 Western countries) organizes help for businesses in Eastern Europe and a similar programme, TACIS, organizes help for the countries of the former Soviet Union.

Apart from these laudable co-operation moves, everyone seemed surprised by the collapse of Communism. Had everyone, especially the members of MI6, the Deuxième Bureau and the CIA, taken the trouble to read Hélène Carrère d'Encausse's admirable book, *L'Empire Eclaté*,[2] published as early as 1978, they would have been fully prepared for this real revolution. In any event, however, apart from the provision of the aforementioned educational and technical assistance, the Community has tended to pay more lip service than to give concrete help to these victims of communism and the former Soviet Empire. True, association agreements have been made with the Visegrad[3] countries and with Bulgaria and Romania and co-operation agreements have been made with the Baltic States and Albania. Unfortunately the trade concessions in general, and those given in these specific agreements in particular, have not been generous. Equally, financial aid has tended to be erratic in nature. It should, however, be added that the EFTA countries have also signed trade agreements with these countries.

Personally, I am of the strongest opinion that we have a deep obligation to help the Eastern European countries and should give them improved trade concessions and greater financial assistance. Having said so much about our desire for democracy in Eastern Europe we are under a moral obligation to help them in their moves toward democracy. Equally, we should support the free trade area agreements made between the Baltic States on the one hand and between the Visegrad countries on the other. Similar agreements between countries of the former Soviet Union should also be encouraged.

Which, if any, of these countries are possible candidates for EC membership? In discussions with my colleague, Professor Robert Farlow of the University of St. Thomas, we came to the conclusion that, at the time of writing, the most likely candidates would be the Czech Republic, Hungary and Poland. I myself would add a major precondition to the criteria for EC membership – but from the side of the present Community. The current EC Member States must be prepared to defend – *militarily* – any future member. This is not an inconsiderable criterion to which we shall return later.

Present and Future Economic and Monetary Policies

Of immediate and urgent concern to all Europeans and, indeed, to all citizens in the world are our current economic and monetary policies. The collapse of the Exchange Rate Mechanism (ERM) of the European Monetary System (EMS) in August this year, through the widening of the bands of fluctuation of EC Member State national currencies to 15 per cent on either side of the central parity, was a salutary watershed in the history of the Community. It is therefore a most opportune moment to review EC economic and monetary policies and to make proposals for the future.

The EC Member States are either 'open' or 'very open' economies and they are conducting 60 per cent of their trade with each other. They have, like many other Western countries, for a number of years now taken the control of inflation as their number one public economic policy goal. They are also the world's most important trade bloc. Consequently, it was both desirable and logical that they should have, as the French had always insisted, their own 'common international monetary personality'. One of the most effective ways to achieve this would be to have an economic and monetary union (EMU) and a common currency. But, apart from certain prerequisites such as similar levels of inflation, such an initiative presupposes a political desire to do so. Furthermore, as we have witnessed, any moves towards a full EMU must be set against changes in the international economic and monetary environment. So, what are the fundamental facts of economic life which we must take into account?

Basically speaking, all trading countries in some way link their currencies with their main trading partners. Small and very open economies always link their currencies and interest rates with those of their main trading partner – e.g. the Netherlands and Germany. In a monetary union, if members really want fixed exchange rates and if they are willing to give total support to each others' currencies, they could beat the speculators. But there would have to be co-ordination of economic and monetary policies. This should have been effective since the Basel/Nyborg Accords of 1987, but has been glaringly absent in recent years from the EMS. The lessons for the future are clear.

Internationally, with the near achievement of the Single European Market (SEM) and the establishment of the European Economic Area (EEA) in late 1993, we should now be set to become the world's superpower. Unhappily, with the present high levels of unemployment and extremely low economic growth, we must examine our internal economic structures and policies.

In anticipation of the SEM there was investment and growth, but there have been and there continue to be major defensive mergers between enterprises both inside and between EC Member States. As Alexis Jacquemin has insisted since the early 1980s, size is no longer an issue for the European Community. Maybe then, we are creating industrial elephants? On the other hand, Pierre-André Buigues,[4] in an erudite study, does cite many examples of sectors where EC countries do possess an important comparative advantage.

More recently, attention has been drawn to the relative inflexibility of the labour market and the high social security (as distinct from health expenses) costs inside EC member states. Similarly, in some countries such as Belgium, the Netherlands and Spain for example, it is almost impossible to dismiss an employee – even where grave professional mistakes are committed. Clearly, such a situation severely reduces the competitive strength of the Community.

Let us imagine, however, that all EC Member States were successfully co-ordinating their economic and monetary policies and their exchange rates were indeed becoming fixed – then what? There is, alas, despite increases in the resources of both the Regional and Social Funds, an obvious shortfall in the transfer of resources between rich and poor regions of the Community, that is, if we are ever to be serious about achieving a full EMU. Furthermore, the regional situation will become much worse if and when the Scandinavian and East European countries join the EC. As Andrew Hughes-Hallet and Andrew Scott [5] have eloquently analysed the situation, this grossly inadequate transfer of funds is the greatest omission in the Treaty on

European Union, which, in contrast, says far too much and too rigidly about conditions for EMU membership. Quite frankly, in this respect the EC does not begin to approach the position of Canada – a loose federation – let alone the United States.

Regarding other policies, we certainly need a greater degree of competition throughout Europe. Concerning the EC and the EEA, the EC Commission which has, despite its lack of experts, performed very well, should be given more teeth and strength to enable it to perform its task of supervising competition policy with improved effectiveness. Equally, to this end, we should improve our levels of education and training (though regarding the latter, Germany and France have accomplished so much), and, as Alexis Jacquemin has so frequently suggested, we should commit ourselves to a policy of 'product differentiation', that is, we should produce and export products more in keeping with our levels of education and technology. In contrast, the CAP, apart from being a gross misallocation of economic resources, condemns us to a third world status. Then, there has to be a greater degree of labour flexibility. Here, the unwarranted levels of social security, taxes and job security in some EC countries reduce our competitive strength. Clearly, where steps have not already been taken to remedy this situation, reforms should be initiated.

Then, as we integrate further it should be easier to achieve an EMU. But, as I have written for over twenty years,[6] in the intervening transitional periods we are concerned with day-to-day balance-of-payments problems. This presents us with a real dilemma. It implies that we need greater regional financial transfers for countries which are poor and/or suffering through the imposition of rigid economic and monetary policies. This would be difficult to achieve. Certainly, as countries are trading, say 70 per cent, of their GDP with each other, they do constitute a *de facto* EMU. The United States, for example, trades 90 per cent of its GDP with itself. Thus, if we really want an EMU, we need more integration, a greater co-ordination of economic and monetary policies, a greater commitment to fixed exchange rates – and an increase in regional financial transfers.

In the meantime, some EC Member States which are already highly integrated with their neighbours and which, consequently, pursue similar economic and monetary policies, will constitute a core EMU. This is further proof of my vision of a Europe à la carte. In the preamble of the Treaty on European Union there are two major aims – a common foreign policy and a common defence policy leading to a common defence. These are indeed important and laudable aims which require a greater degree of examination.

A Common Foreign Policy?

For some time before the French demand for renegotiating the Blair House Accord, made with the United States in November 1992, the European Community had had a foreign economic policy. This policy was influenced by its internal economic structure and policies – notably its lack of indigenous resources of energy and raw materials and the CAP – as well as by its historical links with its former colonial territories around the world. As the world's greatest trading bloc it had, until August 1993, presented a common front in the series of multilateral trade negotiations, organised in the framework of the GATT. Thus, it has had a clear and fairly consistent economic foreign policy. Although never explicitly laid down, it will, as was demonstrated in the case of the Falklands War, guarantee the territorial integrity of EC Member States. However, it wisely does not insist on all states imposing exactly the same sanctions against the enemy. This policy, however, does present us with problems for the future regarding new members of the EC because it is assumed that we must be prepared to guarantee the territorial integrity of these countries. Except in the case of a NATO member like Norway, I am not sure that all are willing to do this. This matter requires the most urgent consideration.

But, now, despite the scandalous débâcle in Bosnia, we aim at a common foreign policy. Happily, this is only an aim and not an obligation. This means, as in the field of military co-operation, that we will have to content ourselves with a selective foreign policy, that is, Europe à la carte, whereby those EC Member States that are willing to undertake joint action will do so. The only binding common foreign policy area will be the trade one. In this context, it is interesting to note that the permanent secretariat of the Council of Ministers (COREPER) will have the 12 permanent representatives 'shadowed' by representatives of the foreign ministries of the 12 Member States. This development does reinforce the role of the Council and tends to exclude the Commission. In the long run, however, as the Community becomes much more integrated, we can expect there to be a common overall foreign policy. In advance of this the reform of the institutions will be imperative. Just as in the United States, Rhode Island could not veto American foreign policy, thus in the EC neither Luxembourg nor the Netherlands would be allowed to veto a common policy. Thus, in exchange for giving up their right of veto (and this is an objective for some time after the year 2000), all countries should have equal representation in a future European Senate as well as, in the immediate future, keeping their right of veto in the Council of Ministers when their vital national interests are at stake.

The Military Dimension

This is indeed the most important and urgent issue at the present time. Because of the demise of Communism we live in troubled and dangerous times in which the one light on the horizon was the agreement by the Ukraine, at the end of August 1993, to finally sell its nuclear warheads and part of the Black Sea fleet to Russia.

We most urgently need a bigger rapid deployment force (RDF) – probably in the framework of the Western European Union (WEU) – as an arm of NATO. Although the idea of the Franco-German Corps is laudable, it is more symbolic than real and will not, in fact, reach its full strength for some time yet. In the meantime, the biggest share of the NATO RDF is borne by Britain. Consequently, other NATO countries should increase their share of this force.

Despite the demise of communism and the major efforts (some already accomplished) by the Americans and Russians to reduce their stockpiles of nuclear weapons, it is imperative that the Europeans should have their own military nuclear capacity – especially if we are to have a common security policy. Furthermore, we do not know what future Russian leaders will be like. Thus, the present Franco-British co-operation in this field should be further encouraged and deepened.

A common defence policy à la carte will be all the more necessary should the neutral Scandinavian countries join the Community. Hitherto, in the case of Ireland, a neutral country, this policy has worked particularly satisfactorily, notably during the Gulf War when only a handful of EC Member States were actively engaged in military activities.

More recently, in the area of defence, there has been much talk of letting East European countries join NATO. Some of these countries certainly believe, rightly or wrongly, that their future safety would be assured in this organization. All will, nevertheless, depend on the attitude of the Russians. A report in *Le Monde*, in August 1993, suggested that Russia would not object to Polish membership of NATO. Certainly, in the long run, an idealistic goal could be to encourage both East European countries *and* Russia to join NATO. Perhaps this is the real guarantee for future peace in Europe. However, many issues such as the Bosnian one would have to be resolved before we could achieve this goal.

The Social Policy Issue

In an attempt to court (successfully, it seems) the British Labour Party, Jacques Delors made the proposal that the Single European Market should be a Community of workers as well as one of employers. Consequently, he proposed the Social Charter [7] which contains, among others, the idea of worker participation in companies (a practice which is widespread in and strongly supported by Germany). This Charter was accepted by all EC Member States except Britain and its main tenets were subsequently included in the Treaty on European Union. The Charter contains many other proposals – including that of 'an equitable wage' about which the Commission has more recently given more details. It is this proposal that gives concern to some economists and politicians who wonder whether the application of this principal might not diminish the Community's international competitiveness. Apart from these proposals, the Charter – like an earlier one put forward by the Council of Europe – sets down the basic rights of workers which should be part of any civilized society.

The Rights of the Citizens:
European Citizenship, Migration and Social Policy

At this stage, I shall be brief and very much to the point. I am not at all sure what is meant by the expression, 'European citizenship'. In contrast, I strongly believe that everyone living within the frontiers of the European Community and all European signatories to the European Convention on Human Rights should enjoy all the freedoms as laid down in that Treaty – that is all, no more and no less. In the light of the present rise of racism and other horrors in Europe, a strict adherence to the tenets as embodied in this Convention becomes a matter of the most urgent European public necessity. Furthermore, an adoption of the economic policies I have outlined above should enable us to provide the means for Europeans to fulfil themselves.

And the Future?

As I said at the outset, my aim in this book is not to forecast the future. Instead, I am attempting to analyse the present situation and to make proposals for the future. But I am sure about one thing, because of our wonderful and irritating national differences we shall never become a United States of Europe. Instead, sometime next century, I foresee the creation of a loose European Confederation – a kind of European Switzerland. In the meantime, except for common policy areas – linked mainly with the achievement of the Single European Market, the CAP (alas), competition and trade policies, some EC Member States and some EFTA countries will integrate more quickly than others and we shall have a situation of Europe à la carte.

A MORE PERSONAL NOTE

But, why this constant and never-ending interest in Europe? As an inhabitant of the ancient and venerable city of York, Europe has been and is always with us. During World War II, for example, a major contingent of the Free French Air Force was stationed in York (in fact, my girlfriend's mother ran off with a Free French Airman). As well as the French, the city positively warmed with the nationals of the occupied European countries. German and Italian prisoners of war, in their leisure time, freely walked the streets of the city. Towards the close of the war, we were appalled to see 15-year-old German prisoners of war arrive at York's railway station.

The end of hostilities did not mean the end of deprivation in Continental Europe. On the contrary, we school children, who had spent the war years collecting money for every conceivable cause, found ourselves in the dreadful winter of 1946–47 morally obliged by our teacher to collect money, clothes and food for the Dutch, who, we were told, were in desperate straits. Shortly after the end of hostilities, York organized pupil exchanges with French and German schools. In this framework, I had the great good fortune to become attached to and to enjoy the incomparable hospitality of the Rousselle family and their friends Lucy Jouanneau and Jean-Pierre Brossmann (now director of the Lyon Opera) in Paris, and, by them, to be introduced to the wonderful French cultural life.

Later at the University of Durham, in the Union Society, I took part in an all-night debate where I led the motion that 'this House believes that the United Kingdom should join the EEC'. When we lost by one vote, I said, 'Now, blindly, you have rejected this motion because you believe that Britain is strong. One day, however, we shall try to enter the Community and the door will be slammed in our faces'. Prophetic words indeed! A year before this debate, in 1956, we were the first British University to organize help for the tragic refugees who were fleeing the brutal and criminal Soviet crushing of the revolt against communism in Hungary. We were able to bring two young Hungarians to study at the University of Durham. When writing my honours dissertation at Durham, I was given generous and detailed advice by that great European, Paul-Henri Spaak, who exemplified traditional Belgian consideration and courtesy. Two years spent in Hamburg enabled me to enjoy the many cultural attractions of that great city and to become acquainted with German literature. In the golden 1970s, I enjoyed the leadership of Hein Schermers at the Europa Instituut, in Amsterdam, before the advent of the 'unacceptable face of Calvinism'. At a more personal level, at the house concerts organized by my

executor, Max Van Egmond, I met, among others, such luminaries as
Guido Pouw and Dennis Van Den Kuyp.

I have then, always lived and breathed Europe, and despite
disappointments, I have faith in the old continent. But, then, as Livio
Missir will exclaim, why no chapter on cultural policy? Because it is
not necessary since we live culture. Whether it is the great literature,
among others, of Britain, France and Germany; the wonderful music
and opera of Germany and Italy; incomparable British theatre; the
unlimited possibilities of seeing great films in Belgium and France – or
just listening to the broadcasts of the BBC International Service each
day – we breath and live culture. It is the rich panoply of cultural
offerings – plus the concern for individuals – that is Europe's great gift
to humanity. It is most important that we protect this heritage.

Amsterdam, Brussels and Minneapolis
July and August, 1993

FOOTNOTE

The main part of this manuscript was completed in the summer of 1993
and a supplement was added in November of the same year. Betweeen
the completion of the manuscript and the receipt of the proofs, many
changes had taken place in Europe. Among these have been NATO's
Partnership for Peace Programme and admission of the four candidates
to the European Union – with Austria's subsequent positive
referendum result.

A development of further relevant interest was the decision taken in
November 1993 by the German Federal Court which determined that
the Treaty on European Union was not, in the framework of Germany's
Constitution, unconstitutional. Thus the Treaty on European Union
became immediately applicable and, apparently, the European
Community (EC) became the European Union (EU). Subsequently
however, the European Court of Justice decreed that since the existing
treaties were still applicable (I presume they mean the Treaties of Paris

and Rome), then the Community (as well as the Union) still exists. Thus the expression was not changed in this text.

Despite these important developments, on the grounds of academic honesty, it was felt wiser not to change the original manuscript.

NOTES

1. In R. Nisbet Bain's erudite work, *The Last King of Poland and his Contemporaries*, originally published in 1909, and then republished in 1971 by the Arno Press and the New York Times, the *liberum veto* is described as being a situation 'whereby any single deputy could explode the Diet, and ipso facto, annul all the previous resolutions, even if they had been voted unanimously'.
2. Hélène Carrère D'Encausse, *L'Empire Éclaté*, Flammarion, Paris, 1978.
3. The Visegrad countries are the Czech and Slovak Republics, Hungary and Poland.
4. P. Buigues, F. Ilzkovitz and J-F Lebrun, *L'Impact Sectoriel Du Marché Intérieur Sur L'Industrie*, Economica, Paris, 1991.
5. A. Hughes-Hallet and A. Scott, 'Fiscal Policy Dilemmas of Monetary Union' in P. Coffey, *Main Economic Policy Areas of the EC — After 1992*, Kluwer Academic Publishers,Dordrecht, 1993.
6. Notably in P. Coffey, *The European Monetary System — Past, Present and Future*, Martinus Nyhoff Publishers, Dordrecht, 1986.
7. It should be noted that the real forerunner of the EC's Social Charter was the European Social Charter of the Council of Europe. This is a more extensive document than its EC counterpart because it does cover important family and migrant issues not included in the Community Social Charter. The Council of Europe Social Charter came into force in February 1965 and was subsequently amended in 1988 and 1991.

1. An Historical Perspective: From Marshall Aid to the Single European Market

THE PRESENT CHOICE

It is certainly no exaggeration to state that Europe finds itself at the most important historical crossroads since 1945. Europe stands before the choice of integration or disintegration – of varying degrees. In particular, the European Community (EC) finds before itself the choice of a much deeper form of integration (as favoured, for very good reasons, by Chancellor Kohl and President Mitterand), or a greater widening of the Community (as favoured by Britain and Denmark for equally valid reasons). On the right choice of integration will depend the fate of Europe for decades to come.

But, before analysing the present choices in greater depth and detail and looking to the future, it is wise to place the present situation in its historical context.

THE HISTORICAL CONTEXT

Today, in contrast with 1945, Europe is unrecognizable. At the end of World War II, with some notable exceptions – such as the cities of Erfurt, Weimar and Prague – all towns with more than 50,000 inhabitants on a latitude from Rotterdam to Moscow were in ruins. In Britain, the centres of nearly all the great industrial cities – as well as the City of London (the financial area) – had been devastated. On top of this destruction, the winter of 1946–47 was the worst in living memory, there was little or no heating and the European transport systems had broken down. As if this was not enough, as soon as hostilities ceased, the generous American Lend-Lease programme of aid ended and European countries were forced to pay for vital American imports with their exports. Then, there was the gradual realization in Western Europe (which the East Europeans were experiencing at first hand) that the Nazi menace had been replaced by the Soviet threat. Over time, the Europeans reacted to these challenges in diverse ways.

Immediate Policy Reactions

Logically, the first reactions – in both Western and Eastern Europe – were military and economic in nature. In an act of great generosity and commitment to Europe, Britain, first in the Treaty of Dunkirk in 1947, and then in the Treaty of Brussels in 1948 (which led to the creation of the Western European Union or WEU), agreed to keep her troops on the Continent of Europe for a period of 50 years. The creation of the WEU also influenced the setting up of the North Atlantic Treaty Organization (NATO) the following year.

But, as has already been mentioned, apart from the Soviet threat, the challenge of the greatest urgency to Europe was that of feeding its citizens and of getting its industries working together. It was then that the United States, in the person of General George Marshall, and with the active support of the Truman Administration, in an act of unparalleled international generosity, set in motion the real moves which were to lead to European integration.[1] Marshall Aid,[2] organized in 1948, was offered to all European countries, including the states of Eastern Europe and the Soviet Union. In fact, Poland and Czechoslovakia did at first accept the American offer but were later persuaded by the Soviets to abandon the project.

The United States made the receipt of this generous financial aid conditional on the Europeans co-operating together and planning the disbursement of the aid among themselves. For this purpose, the Organization for European Economic Co-operation (OEEC) was set up in Paris (it was the forerunner of the present OECD – Organization for

Economic Co-operation and Development). A little later, the European Payments Union (EPU) was also created. This latter and very useful organization lasted until 1958 when it was (in my view) prematurely disbanded. Through the work of both these organizations the Europeans gained valuable experience in co-operating together. In the specific case of the future Federal Republic of Germany (FRG) – or West Germany – the effectiveness of Marshall Aid was reinforced by the extremely successful and prudent currency reform of 1948, which, alas, was not emulated when the the former East Germany was integrated with the FRG at the beginning of the 1990s.

It is sometimes forgotten that the earliest and most profound move toward European integration on a wider scale did in fact come from the former Soviet Union and the countries of Eastern Europe – as a reaction against Marshall Aid. Rightly, or wrongly, the Soviet Union saw this aid as an economic and political threat. Consequently in 1949, the Soviets persuaded their neighbours to create a co-operation agreement, the Council for Mutual Economic Co-operation (CMEA) – or COMECON as observers in the West have called it. This organization did provide the East Europeans with a captive market in the Soviet Union, but, as we shall see later in this book, was finally detrimental to their economic and political development.

Pan-Europeanism: The Council of Europe and its Adjacent Organs

Although the CMEA was a regional reaction to Marshall Aid, there were created, in the same year, 1949, Pan-European bodies dedicated to the defence of human rights. These institutions, with their seat in Strasburg, France, created the European Convention on Human Rights, which was signed on 4 November 1950 and which came into force on 3 September 1953.

Since that date a number of additional protocols have been signed and have come into force. Also, the European Social Charter was signed on 18 October 1961 and came into force on 26 February 1965. In the framework of the Council of Europe are the European Commission of Human Rights and the European Court of Human Rights. There are now 29 Member States in Eastern and Western

Europe of the Council of Europe – who are contracting parties to the European Convention on Human Rights. The Council of Europe – to which I shall return later in this book – could be the best instrument for politically re-integrating Eastern European countries into the West.

Trans-Atlantic Military Co-operation: NATO

Although a number of West European countries had reacted together to create an instrument of common defence in setting up the WEU, it was clear to Britain – notably in the person of then foreign secretary, Ernest Bevin – that a weakened Europe could not stand alone militarily against the Soviet Union. In his fears and with the bringing on stream of Marshall Aid, together with the assumption by the United States of Britain's military role in Greece, torn by a bitter civil war between communists and monarchists, Ernest Bevin found a willing listener in the person of the American President, Harry Truman. It was thanks to the joint efforts of these two men that the North Atlantic Treaty Organization (NATO) was created in 1949. The philosophy of NATO was very simple – a military attack on any one member would be regarded as an attack on all. Its counterpart in Eastern Europe, the Warsaw Pact, was created in 1955 and has now, like the CMEA, ceased to exist. NATO and the WEU are the only remaining military organizations in Western Europe. As with the Council of Europe, I believe (as we shall see later) that they have an important role to play in the future.

Reconciliation between France and Germany

For centuries the French and Germans had been fighting each other and had succeeded in inflicting humiliation and destruction on each other. When World War II came to an end, France, like many other European countries, vowed that Germany should never again regain its former strength and should certainly never be re-armed. As has already been observed, the Treaties of Dunkirk and Brussels had originally aimed at preventing any re-emergence of Naziism and German militarism. By 1949, however, the situation had changed. Germany had been divided into two independent states, the Federal German Republic (West Germany) and the German Democratic Republic (East Germany). An Iron Curtain had fallen between Eastern and Western Europe and the Soviet military and political threat had replaced any potential danger from Germany. Consequently, apart from helping the nascent democracy in West Germany economically through the immediate provision of post-war aid from Britain, US Marshall Aid and the subsequent creation of the OEEC, it was also necessary to integrate that country both economically and politically much more firmly into Western Europe.[3] This view was strongly shared by Chancellor Konrad Adenauer. It was however the French foreign minister Robert Schuman who, in a stroke of genius, made the historic proposal that was to lead to the creation of a community and allow just such a form of deep co-operation to be the real originator of integration in Europe. Robert Schuman's proposal was both simple and revolutionary – European nations should pool the means of war (in the 1950s, coal and steel) under supranational European control. He thus proposed the creation of a European Coal and Steel Community (ECSC) for which membership would be open to all European countries. The following year, 1951, six countries [4] signed the Treaty of Paris which brought the ECSC into being. In the first of a persistent series of oversights, which in total can only be described as a practice of 'missing the European boat', Britain was only represented in this organization by an observer.

Today, it is difficult to comprehend the really revolutionary nature of the ECSC. At that time, the memories of the war were still fresh and there existed considerable animosity towards and fear of Germany. Thus, it was a major achievement to persuade the wartime antagonists to overcome their differences and to co-operate constructively together in the ECSC. Later, in 1963, thanks to the efforts of President de Gaulle and Chancellor Adenauer, a co-operation treaty was signed between France and Germany.

Further Steps towards Reconciliation: Defence

With the division of Germany into two separate and independent states and the increasing fear of a political and military threat from the Soviet Union, it became ever more imperative to anchor the young West

Germany into Western Europe even more firmly. It was agreed among the members of the WEU that defence against the Soviets would be largely ineffective without the active participation of the Germans. Consequently, the Member States of the ECSC agreed to set up a European Defence Force (EDF) under supranational European control and that West Germany would be a member. A European Defence Treaty was signed but was rejected by the French Chamber of Deputies in 1954. The French feeling was that, since Britain had refused to place her independent atomic force and defences under supranational European control, there was no reason why France should do so. However, the vote in the French Parliament created a major crisis because it stopped the moves toward European integration squarely in their tracks. Since it was clear that Western Europe – but especially Britain and France – was totally unready for any form of political union (a theme dear to Jean Monnet) it was felt that some form of economic integration would be more palatable to Western European citizens. It was with this aim in mind that representatives of interested countries in Western Europe were invited to attend a meeting in Messina in 1955.

Transforming a Defeat into Victory – Towards a European Common Market

For many reasons, it is sad and disquieting that Britain was not represented at Messina in 1955 because the participating countries at that conference, the ECSC Member States, agreed to move towards the creation of a customs union and a common market. Furthermore, the subsequent Spaak Report led to the drafting of the Treaty of Rome in which the countries belonging to the ECSC actively participated. In fact, when one examines the Rome Treaty, apart from the basic aims which one associates with a customs union and a common market, it is clear that there was a special something extra (in the affixed procotols) for the founder Member States of the future European Economic Community (EEC). A most notable example here is the series of arrangements made for the overseas territories of the Treaty's signatories. Later members were forced to accept the Treaty as a *'fait accompli'*, including the Common Agricultural Policy (CAP) and the subsequent *acquis communautaires* (Community gains or achievements). As the French rightly say, 'the absent ones are always wrong'.

Alternatives to the EEC

The fact that the six members of the ECSC were the only founder Member States of the EEC clearly implied that many European countries were not only unprepared for a political union, but were not even ready for a more advanced form of economic integration as implied by a customs union or a common market. Apart from entering into preferential or non-preferential trade agreements with other countries, the two other main but more moderate forms of economic integration choices open to Europeans were a free trade area or a co-operation agreement. Since the latter type of arrangement is better suited to countries which are at a less advanced stage of economic development, the free trade area type of agreement clearly appealed to a country like Britain, anxious to keep its Commonwealth preferences. Furthermore, whilst Britain had, for several centuries, clearly demonstrated its commitment to Europe in the military sphere (reinforced by the Treaties of Dunkirk and Brussels), she was totally unwilling to accept Churchill's proposals for a United States of Europe. Instead, apart from the just-mentioned military involvement in Europe, her preference was for a free trade arrangement. Such a trade agreement also appealed to the Scandanavian countries as well as to Austria, Portugal and Switzerland. Apart from the advantages of free trade – without too much economic integration – the seven founder Member States of the European Free Trade Association (EFTA) [5] also wished to have a collective negotiating position *vis-à-vis* the EEC. Equally, it is possible that, in the case of some countries, political considerations about their traditions of neutrality influenced their preference for EFTA membership.

Because the countries of Eastern Europe were artificially cut off from the West, they had to find some kind of trading organization suitable to their conditions – without necessarily giving up any of their remaining political sovereignty. With the exceptions of

Czechoslovakia and East Germany, countries which had reached very high levels of economic development, many countries in Eastern Europe were ideal candidates for the co-operation arrangement or agreement which the Soviet Union proposed for them. The outcome was the creation, in 1949, of the Council for Mutual Economic Assistance (CMEA) – better known in the West as COMECON. Although these countries had a captive market in the Soviet Union and were, for a number of years, to import supplies of energy from that source at very low (by world standards) prices, in the long run this dependence turned out to be a poisoned gift since there was little emphasis on quality and prices were artificially fixed. Together with the inconvertibility of national currencies, this meant that the CMEA Member States were cut off from world trade with all the attendant consequences. To remedy this defect, some countries, notably Hungary in the 1980s, attempted to switch some of their trade to the West.

THE EUROPEAN COMMUNITY – TOWARDS THE SINGLE EUROPEAN MARKET

Just as the United States is not the Americas, the European Community is not Europe. However, in both cases they are the economic motors for their continents. Inevitably then, they are poles of attraction for their neighbours. Indeed, in the case of the EC, as we shall observe later in this work, not only have some of the former members of EFTA joined the Community, but most of the remaining ones are currently in the process of negotiating their membership or are actively considering this possibility. So, what are the reasons for the EC's apparent irresistible attraction for other countries? The answer to this question lies in the increasing importance of the EC internationally and its potential political and economic strength. Although the Community has experienced (and continues to experience) disappointments, the temptation for European countries (especially the smaller ones) to have a voice in the EC Council of Ministers is indeed great. As we shall see in the next section, in some areas the EC has exceeded expectations, in others it has disappointed its admirers.

The Evolution of the European Community (EEC)

The proof of the success of the EEC (named the European Community, EC, as from February 1993), is shown in the numbers of Member States[7] which have increased from six to twelve. At the outset, the goals of the EEC were rather modest and could be summed up as being the creation of a customs union and a partial common market. In the list of aims laid down in the preamble of the Treaty of Rome (see below), there was no mention of industrial, energy, monetary and regional policies. Also, in the Treaty itself there was talk of merely approximating fiscal policies, and later it was agreed that these would only cover sales and corporation taxes, and excise duties.

The six founder Member States did, in some major areas, achieve their aims ahead of the deadline set down in the transitional period, 1958-70.[8] Thus, for example, the tariff and quantitative restrictions on the internal movement of goods had been removed and a common external tariff (CET) put in place by 1968. In contrast no progress at all had been made regarding the establishment of a common transport policy, the free movement of capital and the establishment of services. The Community had to wait until the 1980s and the 1990s to make progress in these areas. But the first decade of the Community's life was wonderful indeed! Investment poured into the area, economic growth was exceptional, the EEC Member States became more integrated among themselves (by 1970, they were conducting half of their trade among themselves), and in the Kennedy Round of Multilateral Trade Negotiations (MTNs) held within framework of the General Agreement on Tariffs and Trade (GATT) the Community became the great protagonist *vis-à-vis* the United States. . . These were indeed halcyon days! Small wonder, then, that the United Kingdom and other European countries felt that they had to be in this exclusive and powerful club in which, should they find it absolutely necessary, they could always use their right of veto in the Council of Ministers.[9] The much smaller Benelux countries had long since understood that they would be nothing outside the EEC whereas inside the club they would have an influence out of all proportion to their size. The basic aims of the EEC during this period (1958–1970) were:

1. Removal of tariffs and quantitative restrictions on internal movement of goods.

2. Establishment of a common external tariff (CET) and common commercial policy towards third parties.

3. Removal of obstacles toward movement of persons, goods, capital and services.

4. Establishment of a Common Agricultural Policy (CAP).

5. Establishment of a Common Transport Policy.

6. Establishment of a system ensuring that competition would not be distorted.

7. Co-ordination of economic policies of Member States and remedying balance of payments disequilibria.

8. Approximation of respective municipal law.

9. Creation of a European Social Fund.

10. Establishment of a European Investment Bank.

11. The association of overseas territories and countries with the Community, with a view to increasing trade and to pursuing jointly their efforts towards economic and social development.

Before Britain, Denmark and Ireland signed their Membership Treaty in 1972, they had insisted that something should be done for their EFTA partners. Thus, bilateral free trade agreements (excepting agricultural and some other products) were signed between the Community and each EFTA Member State. Consequently, Western Europe has, for some time, had a huge free trade area. Alas, when the three new Members joined, they had not anticipated the ensuing energy and economic crises, and, whatever economic growth there was, it could not be compared with the explosion of the 1960s. Also, the faltering first steps of the Community to create an economic and monetary union (EMU) through the introduction of the 'Snake in the Tunnel' and the 'Snake Arrangement' (to be discussed in Chapter 3) could hardly be described as being successful. Then, as if all this was not enough, there was, in the 1980s, talk of 'Euro-sclerosis' with the attendant fear that the United States (partly through its Star Wars Project) and Japan would surpass the EEC technologically. Equally, it had for some time been realized that the aims of a Common Market had not been achieved.[10] All experts agreed that the trade effects of a customs union were once and for all. However, the dynamic effects of a common market – such as economies of scale, long production runs and specialization – could only be achieved in a large internal market (cf. the United States) unimpeded by non-tariff barriers. It was with this mind that the Commission published its white paper on the Single European Market in 1985.

The Single European Market

The signing of the Single European Act in 1986 which became law in July 1987 when the Irish, in a referendum, approved the document, did not cause a single ripple of interest anywhere. It was only after the publication of a major Commission report, headed by Paolo Cecchini, on the 'Costs of non-Europe' that '1992' became the obsession of nearly everyone both inside and outside the Community. In reality, 1992 was only a goal and not a definitive date. To bring on stream a Single European Market (SEM), 282 directives had to be accepted by the Council of Ministers and most of them had to be 'transposed' into national law before they would become European law.

Progress and Problems

The state of play with these directives, as reported in *Europe* of Agence Europe, on 14 June 1993, is as follows. The number of directives 'legally' in force total 258, 214 of which require 'transposition'. Denmark, Italy and Britain are the most diligent Member States in transposing these measures, see Table 1.1.

Much progress has been achieved and there have also been disappointments. Some of the success stories were unexpected. Thus, compromises were reached regarding the levels of value added tax (VAT) and the opening up of public procurement to competitive bidding in a number of major areas. Much progress has been made in the mutual recognition of degrees, diplomas and professional qualifications. Moves have been made to adopt common standards but

Table 1.1 *Directives transposed into national legislation*

	Measures transposed	Derogations	Measures not transposed	Not relevant
Belgium	184	0	25	6
Denmark	197	0	11	7
Germany	166	0	43	6
Greece	159	2	49	5
Spain	172	2	38	3
France	178	0	32	5
Ireland	167	1	41	6
Italy	191	0	20	4
Luxembourg	174	0	33	8
Netherlands	173	0	36	6
Portugal	177	2	34	2
U.K.	189	1	19	6

Source: Agence Europe, 14 June 1993

the present trend is, alas, to recognize each other's standards. In the field of financial services a common European banking passport was introduced, as planned, on 1 January 1993. In 1994, the same (with some *derogations* or temporary exemptions) will apply for insurance and, as from 1996, for stockbroking.

In contrast, no progress at all was made with a common transport policy (trucking). In June 1993 it was agreed that we shall have such a policy in 1998. The same deadline (with *derogations* for four Member States) goes for opening up the internal telecommunications markets of Member States. Regarding the opening up of the internal energy markets, we shall have to wait until the next century. In December 1993 the nine signatories of the Schengen Agreement (all Member States except Britain, Denmark and Ireland) were to have removed internal passport controls. But we shall have to wait until 1998 for a complete deregulation of the airlines industry.

From the market viewpoint, the really important achievement is the European Economic Area (EEA) between the EC and EFTA Member States (with the exception of Switzerland) which will come into effect on 1 January 1994. Without wishing to indulge in platitidues, this creates the most important internal market in the world. Apart from cultural, political and social considerations, this is the great economic attraction for countries in Eastern Europe.

NOTES

1. For the sake of historical accuracy it should be stated that the representatives of the free Benelux Governments had agreed, in London, in the war years, to form a union among themselves when hostilities were over. This was a logical move since Belgium and the Netherlands had, until the early 1830s, been ruled as one country for many years. The outcome was the creation, in 1948, of the Benelux Union.
2. The financial aid disbursed under the Marshall Plan amounted to $12.5 billion (about $70 million in today's figures) and the recipient countries were as follows: Austria, Netherlands, Ireland, France, Norway, Italy, Iceland, Denmark, West Germany, Britain, Luxemburg, Belgium and Sweden.
3. It is important to note that the Western allies accepted that trade between the two Germanies should be considered as 'internal German trade'. This agreement was continued by the EEC.
4. These countries, which were also to be the founder Member States of the European Economic Community (EEC), were Belgium, France, Germany (West), Italy, Luxemburg and the Netherlands.
5. These countries were Austria, Britain, Denmark, Norway, Portugal, Sweden and Switzerland. The EFTA, which came into being in 1960, was based on the Treaty of Stockholm, 1963.
6. The original members of the CMEA were Albania, Bulgaria, Czechoslovakia, Hungary, East Germany (GDR), Poland and the Soviet Union. However, associate member and/or observer status was given to three non-European countries: Cuba, Mongolia and Vietnam.
7. The six founder Member States of the EC (see: note 4 above) have since been joined by Britain, Denmark, Greece, Ireland, Portugal and Spain.
8. It should be noted that new Member States are generally given a transitional period of about five years (with some exceptions for specific sections) to adopt the aims laid down in the Treaty – plus the intervening *acquis communautaires* (Community gains or achievements).
9. Following the 'Luxemburg Compromise', agreed upon in 1966 – on French (General de Gaulle's) insistence – when a Member State believes that its vital national interests will be at stake through an EEC policy decision, it has the right to say so and to use its right

of veto in the Council of Ministers. This right is still very much alive, and, for example, Luxemburg has threatened to use this right should the Community try to introduce an EC withholding tax.

10. Indeed, this fact had already been observed at the end of the 1960s and the early 1970s by Colonna and Spinelli.

2. Earlier Attempts at Political Co-operation: Common Foreign and Security Policies

My first chapter does, perhaps erroneously, give the impression that, in the early years of the life of the EEC, the principal concern was with economic matters and that, in the Community, there was little or no interest in political co-operation between EC Member States or in the formulation of common foreign and security policies. In reality, nothing could be further from the truth. A strong movement in favour of political co-operation had, in fact, started at the end of 1960 and culminated in the creation of the Fouchet Committee and Plan before its author was packed off to Algeria as Governor-General by President de Gaulle. But, as in the case of the early attempts to create an EMU – with the Werner Plan compromise between the Economists' (with the Schiller Plan) and the Monetarists' (with the Barre Plans) Schools of thought,[1] and the ensuing 'Snake in the Tunnel' and 'Snake Arrangement' – so, in the case of political co-operation, some background history is essential.

One of the many critical years in the political history of post-war Europe was 1958, the year when the Treaty of Rome ushered in the first stage of the EEC. It was also the year when, under the aegis of the Maudling Committee, Britain and the six EEC Founder Member States were trying to bridge the gap between the British preference for a European trading arrangement and that of the Six for a stronger form of union. Personally, I believe that had Britain played her cards well in 1957 and in the early part of 1958 she would have entered the EEC – with many concessions. All that changed with the return to power of General de Gaulle in 1958. The General made it clear that, if Britain wished to join the Community, she would have to accept the whole of the Treaty of Rome – including the Common Agricultural Policy (CAP).

As is common knowledge, General de Gaulle had many an axe to grind with the Anglo-Saxons. He could not accept, for example, the so-called 'special relationship' between the United States and Britain whereby the Americans shared atomic military secrets with Britain but not with France. Then, he could not accept the dominant role of the dollar (supported by the pound sterling) as the world's reserve asset. Of lesser importance, but emotionally and psychologically very hot, was the increasing use of the English language internationally. The General intended that French would be the working language of the EEC – there was no place for English.

At a larger diplomatic level, and at a later date, he envisaged the *rapprochement* between France and West Germany as a main plank of French foreign policy, once the Algerian crisis was solved. Here, he found a willing partner in Chancellor Adenauer. In the 1970s, Chancellor Schmidt and President Giscard d'Estaing revived this close personal association, and, to this day, this alliance is the cornerstone of French foreign policy.

As already mentioned, the first negotiations for political co-operation between the EEC Member States had started at the end of 1960 – in the framework of the nascent Franco-German co-operation. Early in the following year, President de Gaulle's Foreign Minister, Couve de Murville, had made proposals (obviously with the General's approval) for the holding of regular meetings between Heads of State and Heads of Government which would lead to closer political co-operation between the Member States. Then arose the problem of the nation state or Community organs. Thus, the Netherlands were immediately and strongly opposed to these proposals and subsequent ones made early in 1961 because the Dutch feared, among other reasons, that political decisions might be taken in the Council of Ministers outside the EEC institutional context. Nevertheless, in July of the same year, the Six accepted the 'Bad Godesberg' Declaration whereby, in various policy areas, they would, in principle, move towards a political union in Europe whilst at the same time strengthening the Atlantic Alliance. It was two months later that the special committee, organized by the EEC Heads of State and

Government, met under the chairmanship of the special French representative, Christian Fouchet. The Fouchet Committee studied the points of view of the EEC Member States and then, in October, put forward a draft treaty which, among other aims, did propose the creation of a common foreign and defence policy. These proposals have always fascinated students of politics.

The illusions of France's five EEC partners were abruptly and brutally destroyed when, in January 1962, under strict orders from President de Gaulle, the French delegation proposed a plan for co-operation which was a very much watered down version of the plan put forward by the Fouchet Committee. It was in May of the same year that President de Gaulle made it quite clear that any form of political co-operation in the EEC would have to be between nation states and that the Community institutions would be subservient to them. This is a view that Britain would certainly have supported both then and now.

The Community had to wait until the end of 1964 for the Fouchet Plan to be put once more on the agenda for political co-operation. This time it was proposed by the Federal German Republic and, as on previous occasions, supported by the Netherlands. In contrast, Italy proposed the creation of a permanent secretariat for political co-operation and the strengthening of the powers of the European Parliament.

In a totally different vein, President de Gaulle repeated his proposals for the creation of an independent European defence policy (i.e. independent of the United States). The French, it should be remembered, were strongly opposed to the American proposal (made in 1963) for the creation of a Multilateral Atomic Force.

In view of these profound differences between the EEC Member States, and notably France's opposition to supranationality, no discussions about European political union took place until the end of the 1960s. The Fouchet Plan, which had been welcomed and supported by so many politicians inside and outside the EEC, became another historical document. In the meantime, the Commission's proposals of 1965, which would have increased the budgetary powers of the European Parliament, reduced the influence of the Council and encouraged co-operation between the Commission and the Parliament, encountered the wrath of President de Gaulle. These proposals might have been overlooked by the French had it been possible to arrive at common prices for cereals by 1 July 1965 – when the transitional price arrangements expired. Also, it should be remembered that the Commission had proposed that the Community should have its own financial resources (*resources propres*) on that same date.

This proposal, with its supranational implications, was equally unacceptable to the French. The upshot was France's policy of the empty chair (*chaise vide*) in the Council of Ministers – to which I make frequent reference in this book. It was in January 1966 that the Luxemburg Protocol or Compromise was accepted by the Six. This decision has influenced Community political co-operation (or the lack of it) until this present day and has been used by all Member States. It was a successor to de Gaulle, President Giscard d'Estaing, who, in a modified version, re-introduced the concept of a 'Europe of the Nation States' by the holding of European Summits twice a year.[2] These meetings, surrounded by a great deal of publicity when it seems that the intellectual attention of ministers is limited (in public) to a flash of a few minutes (or seconds) on television, are organized by the national president of the EC Council at the end of the six-month presidency of the country in question. It is, however, questionable to what degree these meetings are really constructive – particularly in the domains of political, foreign policy and defence/security co-operation.

My personal impression is that important decisions relating to items on hidden agendas are taken elsewhere – removed from the glare of publicity. Furthermore, most unfortunately, when a small EC Member State occupies the presidency of the Council of Ministers (as was the situation with the beginnings of the Yugoslav–Bosnian crisis) whenever grave political and foreign policy crises arise, the Community is unprepared to deal with them. This is where the adoption of Alan Sked's proposal for a permanent Council of European Ministers, in Brussels, would be useful.

In examining these early attempts at political co-operation between EEC Member States I have tried to emphasize the profound nationalist and/or supranational feelings among these countries which have persisted until the present day.[3] No amount of wishful thinking will remove these differences. This is one of the main reasons why I believe that it would be wiser for us to adopt a policy of Europe à la carte.

NOTES

1. For a detailed account of the different early plans for an EMU, see: P. Coffey and J.R. Presley, 1970, *European Monetary Integration*, London: Macmillan.
2. For this purpose, the Council is known as the Council of the European Community or the Council of the European Union. The names should not be confused with the Council of Europe, a separate and pan-European institution with its seat in Strasburg.
3. Although I was already fully aware of the events described in this chapter, I have had recourse to the following work in order to firmly establish the precise dates: Hans Von der Groeben, 1984, *Combat Pour L'Europe*, Commission of the European Communities, Brussels.

3. Attempts at Forming an Economic and Monetary Union

Few issues could be more topical and relevant than the European Community's attempts to create an economic and monetary union (EMU). In reality, the EC has had a long and at times tumultuous history in this domain. To the surprise of many of my colleagues, the orginal decision to move along the road to creating an EMU was taken by the Heads of State and Government of the then EEC, in the Hague late in 1969, with the proviso: 'provided that the political will to do so exists'.

But first, what exactly is an EMU? Writing in 1984,[1] I defined it as follows:

> In the case of the members of a customs union, such as the EEC, a full EMU implies the free movement of goods, persons, capital and services within the union – plus the existence of a common external tariff vis-à-vis third parties. It implies irrevocably fixed exchange rates plus full convertibility – or a common currency. Also, it implies common economic, fiscal and monetary policies – together with a minimum degree of fiscal integration. In turn, common monetary policies vis-à-vis third parties would exist. Finally, these implications would presuppose certain common decision making organs such as a central bank, among others, for example.

> Coffey, 1984 and 1987

It should be borne in mind that such an undertaking is, to say the least, arduous and awesome, particularly when it is taken on a voluntary basis. An EMU involves the giving up of an enormous amount of sovereignty because in its final stage, when the national currencies of the participating countries are 'irrevocably' linked together and/or a common currency is introduced, these countries give up their right to use changes in the parities of their currencies to remedy balance-of-payments (BOP) problems. But, equally, BOP disequilibria between these countries disappear and are replaced by regional disequilibria. So, why as early as in 1969, did the original six founder Member States agree to such a momentous undertaking? As I have, on several occasions, observed,[2] there were a number of valid reasons for this decision. These were:

> The EEC Member States had, by 1968, achieved most of the aims as laid down in the Treaty of Rome. Quite simply, ahead of time, the customs union had been achieved. Consequently, the economies of the Member States had become well integrated and they were conducting about half their trade between themselves. Then, there was the position of the Community's Common Agricultural Policy. The successful functioning of this policy depended on stable (preferably fixed) exchange rates. At an international level, the EEC had become the world's most important economic and trading bloc, endowed with the most important reserves of gold and convertible currencies. France had, for a number of years, considered that the Community should consequently be endowed with a 'common international monetary personality'. One of the best ways of demonstrating such a personality would be to create an EMU and a common currency. Also, it should be borne in mind that up to 1968 the western world had experienced a full decade of relatively stable exchange rates. It was hoped that this situation would continue, and one of the best ways of ensuring the continuation of this state of affairs would be to create an EMU.
>
> Coffey, 1984 and 1987

Before examining the early EEC plans for an EMU, their application and the ensuing results – as well as for reasons of theoretical respectability – it is useful to indulge in an historical overview of optium currency areas and economic and/or monetary unions.

AN ECONOMIC AND MONETARY UNION AND/OR AN OPTIMUM CURRENCY AREA

There exists a considerable degree of confusion about an economic and monetary union (EMU) and an optimum currency area (OCA) – which are not necessarily the same thing. When we enter the terrain of OCA theories we are trying to provide ourselves with theoretical yardsticks which will help us to determine which countries should link their currencies together and possibly create an EMU. There are many definitions of OCAs – nearly all of which were formulated in the old days of Bretton Woods when fixed or stable exchange-rates were the norm and when the amounts of 'hot money' floating round the world were considerably less than is presently the case.

Despite these reservations, one can recognize certain basic criteria, which, where they exist, could constitute an OCA. Thus, there exists a consensus of opinion among many economists that:

(i)   small, very 'open' economies should link their currencies with their main trading partner (s);

(ii) where factors of production move freely between countries as an equilibriating factor, these countries could constitute an OCA.

(iii) In the 1970s, Giovanni Magnifico coined a new definition for an OCA, 'a similar propensity to inflate'.

(iv) Perhaps not quite an OCA is the so-called 'portfolio approach' whereby one or more countries will continue to buy up the treasury bills, bonds and currencies of their trading partner(s) on a fairly limitless basis.

Personally, I discern a combination of currents which could enable some countries to form an OCA, a monetary union or even an EMU. I will use historical and current examples to support my case.

There are good examples to support the first criterion on this list. Thus, when Ireland became independent from England, it chose to link its currency with the pound sterling, and in reality a monetary union, but not an EMU, existed between the two countries. Early in the 1970s, however, I wrote that when that country conducted an equal amount or more of its trade with its other EEC partners it would break its links with the pound sterling and link its currencies with other EC Member States. This did in fact happen. The example of the Netherlands and Germany is another example of a small, very open economy linking its currency to that of its main trading partners. The currencies of the two countries have been closely linked since shortly after World War II. But, they also have a 'fairly similar propensity to inflate'. Another example is that of Luxemburg and Belgium, between which countries a monetary union has existed since the early 1920s. Here, however, the excessively heavy Belgian public debt is threatening to destroy the monetary union between them. Historically speaking, the example of Scotland and England is the best case of both an OCA and an EMU between two trading partners of very different sizes. It would be illogical for the Scots to withdraw from this union – though I think they should have a greater degree of political autonomy.

How relevant are the second and third criteria to situations today? Logically, there must exist the equilibriating element as constituted by the free movement of factors of production between regions and/or countries which could be eligible to consitute an OCA. Equally, the criterion of inflation is important in an international context.

Using the second set of criteria, do, for example, the EC and the USA constitute OCAs? Apparently not. Whilst the EC has, for some time, allowed labour to move freely within the Community, and there now exists mutual recognition for most qualifications, EC workers are not mobile. By early 1992, capital had been moving freely between all the EC Member States except Greece, and we are (here we have advanced more than the USA) well on the way to freeing the establishment of financial services throughout the Community. Goods have, for some time, moved freely inside the EC and the compromise reached on value added tax (VAT) should help to remove existing barriers. Even more so than in the United States, considerable regional income differentials exist inside the Community.

The United States does permit the free movement of all its factors of production except financial services. Here, banking and insurance are conducted at the state level and not at the federal one. In contrast, labour is highly mobile. As with the EC, income disparities exist across the regions, though they are less extreme than those in the Community. What, I believe, makes the USA a better OCA than the EC is the fact that it does conduct about 90 per cent of its trade between its own internal regions and that labour and capital are highly mobile equilibriating factors. Also, price differentials are not great across the country and there are important federal financial transfers between the regions. Thus, the US is a much better candidate as an EMU than is the EC.

EARLIER PLANS FOR AN EMU

It will be remembered that there were as many as four official plans for an EMU at the end of the 1960s. These were the Schiller Plan, the two Barre Plans and the Werner Plan. The Schiller Proposals embodied the beliefs of the Economists' School – as supported by West Germany and the Netherlands – whilst the Barre Plans embodied the beliefs of the Monetarists' School – as supported by France.   There existed tremendous intellectual friction between the two schools of thought and it was for this reason that, at the meeting of EC finance ministers held in Venice in May 1970, Monsieur Werner of Luxemburg was invited to prepare a second and definitive report which would be a kind of compromise plan between the two parties. It was in this plan, published in October 1970,[3] wherein lie the roots of the present European Monetary System (EMS).

The report erred more on the side of the Monetarists [4] than on that of the Economists in that the plan proposed a narrowing of the margins of fluctuation around the central parity of the EEC currencies from the 1.5 per cent for the US dollar to 1.2 per cent – hence the description of the EEC 'Snake in the (US dollar) Tunnel' (see Figure 3.1). Following the widening of the margin of fluctuation for the US dollar to 4.5 per cent, at the Smithsonian Agreement at the end of 1971, the EEC margin was widened to 2.25 per cent (see Figure 3.2). It is this margin of fluctuation which has also been the basis of the European Monetary System (EMS). Because of the international monetary upheavals, the 'Snake in the Tunnel' mechanism did not last long. It came into being in April 1972 and lasted for about a year. On March 12, 1973, it was replaced by the 'Snake Arrangement' and the participating countries organized a joint float against the US dollar.

Figure 3.1   The 'Snake in the Tunnel' arrangement as proposed the Werner Plan in 1970

1.2% EEC
National
currencies
'Snake'

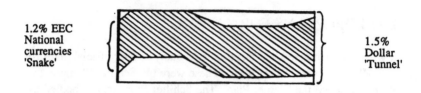

1.5%
Dollar
'Tunnel'

Source: P. Coffey, Main Economic Policy Areas of the EEC, Den Haag: Nijhoff, 1983.

Figure 3.2   The proposed 'Snake in the Tunnel' arrangement following the Smithsonian agreements in 1971

2.25% EEC
National
Currencies
'Snake'

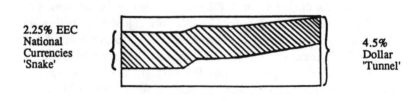

4.5%
Dollar
'Tunnel'

Source: P. Coffey, Main Economic Policy Areas of the EEC, Den Haag: Nijhoff, 1983.

The experience of this monetary reptile was not a happy one. Britain's membership (like that of Ireland's) lasted two months, during which time we lost about a third of our reserves. Denmark left the Arrangement and then returned whilst France left it, returned, and then, once again, departed. For most of the time Norway and Sweden were associated with the Arrangement. At the end of its life, the Snake Arrangement comprised a Deutsche Mark zone consisting of West Germany, the Benelux countries and Denmark.

What went wrong with the system? Changes (currency re-alignments) came too late and were generally inadequate. Italy said she would have remained in the Arrangement had generous credits been available. Then, the 'Snake' Arrangement was sailing against international monetary storms. Nevertheless, things could not stay as they were. The EEC Member States were and are major trading nations, which in the long run do not function well with long-term international currency upheavals. Furthermore, the public declarations of two American Presidents that they couldn't care less about the value of the US dollar did nothing to reassure the Europeans. It was thus that Chancellor Schmidt and President Giscard d'Estaing got together and took up Roy Jenkins's proposals for the creation of a European Monetary System (EMS) in which the kingpin would be the European Currency Unit (ECU).

THE EUROPEAN MONETARY SYSTEM (EMS)

The EMS bears some similarity to its predecessor, the Snake Arrangement, but it also embodies fundamentally key differences which could serve as an example for other countries – especially those embarking upon similar forms of economic and monetary union. Technically speaking, there are two elements to the EMS, the Grid or bilateral national currency to national currency mechanism, and the more constricting Exchange Rate Mechanism (ERM), i.e. the national currency to the ECU (European Currency Unit) link (see Figure 3.3).

Figure 3.3 The Grid System

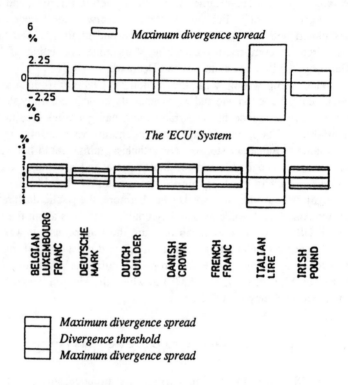

Divergence Threshold: When a currency reaches the upper or lower limits of this band, the Government concerned must intervene in the currency markets.

Source: P. Coffey, 'The European Monetary System – Six Months Later', *Three Banks Review*, London: December 1979.

In the case of the former, the same margin of fluctuation, i.e. 2.25 per cent, is operated as under the Snake Arrangement. However, in the earlier case, Italy, and in the more recent cases of Britain, Portugal and Spain, a wider margin of 6 per cent is in operation. In the case of the ERM, the Commission has individualized the margins of fluctuation *vis-à-vis* the ECU (see Table 3.1). The ECU itself is a basket of the 12 currencies of the EC Member States as shown below as on 23 November 1992:

Deutsche Mark	31.69%
French Franc	20.16%
Pound Sterling	10.90%
Dutch Guilder	9.90%
Italian Lira	8.98%
*Belgian Franc	8.44%
Spanish Peseta	4.80%
Danish Crown	2.63%
Irish Pound	1.16%
Portuguese Escudo	.76%
Greek Drachma	.57%

* Includes the Luxemburg Franc

The narrow, in some cases extremely narrow, margins of fluctuation *vis-à-vis* the ECU (all Member States except Greece participated in the ERM) are a constraint on the members of the ERM. Even more constrictive are the following four commitments that Member States accept on joining this active part of the EMS whenever their currencies come under pressure.

Thus, the responsibilities of the country concerned when the Divergence Indicator is reached *vis-à-vis* the ECU by its currency are clearly laid down by the Resolution of the Council of Ministers of 5 December 1978. They are:

1. diversified intervention
2. monetary measures
3. drawing on credit facilities
4. external and domestic policy measures

Table 3.1 *The Commission's 'individualization' of maximum divergence spreads and divergence thresholds*

Currencies	Maximum divergence threshold spread *vis-à-vis* the ECU (as of 21 Nov. 1992) %	Divergence threshold *vis-à-vis* the ECU (until 16 Sept.1984) %	Divergence threshold after 16 Sept. 1984 %
Belgian/Luxem. Franc	2.06	1.52	1.543
Deutsche Mark	1.54	1.13	1.146
Dutch Guilder		1.51	1.516
Danish Crown	2.19	1.64	1.642
French Franc	1.80	1.35	1.366
Italian Lira	—	4.07	4.051
Irish Pound	2.22	1.67	1.667
Pound Sterling	—	—	—
Portuguese Escudo	5.95		
Spanish Peseta	5.71		

These commitments are indeed a salutary lesson for other countries, notably the United States. In detail, they imply that when a participating country's currency comes under pressure on the exchange markets, that country – and the other countries whose currencies are concerned – will intervene on the markets in an attempt to remedy the situation. If this action fails, then the country concerned will raise or lower interest rates. It then may have recourse to the generous short and medium-term credits available under the EMS. If all these three sets of action are of no avail, then the country concerned will be obliged to take internal and external economic action, normally of a fiscal nature. Finally, if all this fails to improve the position of the currency under pressure, a swift and discreet exchange rate re-alignment may have to be operated. All in all, these are indeed major commitments which have been voluntarily accepted by these countries. Furthermore, they were supplemented by the Basel/Nyborg Agreement of 1987 to co-ordinate economic and monetary policies. To underline the role of the ECU, all 12 Member States exchanged 20 per cent of their reserves of gold and US Dollars for official ECUs.

In comparison with its predecessor, the EMS had, until 1992, been successful. No participant had left the system whilst three new countries, Britain, Spain and Portugal, had joined the ERM. Although no further allocations of official ECUs have been created and the EMS did not move on to a second stage – as had been planned – in March 1981, the unplanned creation and expansion of the commercial ECU market has been very successful. There has been an expansion in commercial inter-bank deposits and a number of EC governments have made major issues of ECU denominated treasury bills, securities and bonds. It is possible also to buy ECU-denominated travellers' cheques and to open up ECU-denominated private bank accounts. In some countries, ECU coins are accepted as legal tender. Most important of all, the ECU has remained more stable than other units of account or currencies and the EMS has constituted an important zone of monetary stability.

It was perhaps a combination of this stability – together with the desire, notably by Jacques Delors, for a greater degree of integration, which led to the creation of the Committee on EMU and the publication of the report bearing Jacques Delors' name in April of 1989. Like the subsequent Treaty on European Union, this report called for the creation of an EMU in three stages – leading also to the creation of a single currency and an independent central bank. It also called for convergence between the economies of the participating countries, and, in the second stage, for a narrowing of the band of fluctuation around the participating currencies to one per cent. Although the beginning of the first stage was set for 1990, no dates were given for the other stages.

The major currency upheavals, which started in the summer of 1992 and which led to the departure of Britain and Italy from the Exchange

Rate Mechanism (ERM) of the EMS, continued into the summer of 1993. The result was that only Germany and the Netherlands remained in the band of fluctuation of 2.25 per cent whilst a margin of 15 per cent was organized for the remaining participating countries. In contrast with the earlier success of the EMS, all this constituted a débâcle. What went wrong and could this collapse have been avoided? These points and possible future policies are examined in Chapter 9.

THE RECORD OF THE EUROPEAN MONETARY SYSTEM

13 March 1979
Introduction of the EMS

23 September 1979
Adjustments within the EMS:
5 per cent re-evaluation of the Deutsche Mark *vis-à-vis* the Danish Krone
2 per cent re-evaluation of the Deutsche Mark *vis-à-vis* the Belgian, French and
　　Luxemburg Francs, Dutch Guilder, Italian Lira and the Irish Punt

27 November 1980
5 per cent devaluation of the Danish Krone

23 March 1981
6 per cent devaluation of the Italian Lira

4 October 1981
5.5 per cent revaluation of the Deutsche Mark and the Dutch Guilder
3.5 per cent devaluation of the French Franc and the Italian Lira

21 February 1982
8.5 per cent devaluation of the Belgian Franc
3 per cent devaluation of the of the Danish Krone

12 June 1982
4.25 per cent revaluation of the Deutsche Mark and the Dutch Guilder
5.75 per cent devaluation of the French Franc
2.75 per cent devaluation of the Italian Lira

21 March 1983
5.5 per cent revaluation of the Deutsche Mark
3.5 per cent revaluation of the Dutch Guilder
2.5 per cent revaluation of the Danish Krone
1.5 per cent revaluation of the Belgian/Luxemburg Franc
2.5 per cent devaluation of the French Franc and the Italian Lira
3.5 per cent devaluation of the Irish Punt

21 July 1985
6 per cent devaluation of the Italian Lira
2 per cent revaluation of the Deutsche Mark, the Dutch Guilder, the Danish
    Krone, the Belgian/Luxemburg Franc, the French Franc and the Irish Punt

7 April 1986
3 per cent revaluation of the Deutsche Mark and Dutch Guilder
1 per cent revaluation of the Belgian/Luxemburg Franc and the Danish Krone
3 per cent devaluation of the French Franc

4 August 1986
8 per cent devaluation of the Irish Punt

12 January 1987
3 per cent revaluation of the Deutsche Mark and Dutch Guilder
2 per cent revaluation of the Belgian/Luxemburg Franc

19 June 1989
Spanish Peseta enters the EMS under the wide band of ±6 per cent

5 January 1990
Italian Lira moves to the narrow band of ± 2.25 per cent
3.5 per cent devaluation of the Italian Lira

5 October 1990
British Pound enters the EMS under the wide band of ±6 per cent

6 April 1992
Portuguese Escudo enters the EMS under the wide band of ±6 per cent

13 September 1992
7 per cent devaluation of the Italian Lira.
Italian Lira membership is suspended

16 September 1992
British Pound membership is suspended

17 September 1992
5 per cent devaluation of the Spanish Peseta

22 November 1992
6 per cent devaluation of the Spanish Peseta
6 per cent devaluation of the Portuguese Escudo

1 February 1993
10 per cent devaluation of the Irish Punt

13 May 1993
8 per cent devaluation of the Spanish Paseta
6.5 per cent devaluation of the Portuguese Escudo

2 August 1993
All ERM currencies allowed to fluctuate by 15 per cent (except the German and
Dutch currencies which continue to fluctuate in the old margin of 2.25 per cent)
Drachma, Lira and Sterling still floating

NOTES

1.   P. Coffey, 1984 and 1987, *The European Monetary System – Past, Present and Future,*
     Dordrecht: Kluwer Academic Publishers.

2. P. Coffey, op. cit.
3. Commission of the European Communities, 1970, 'Report to the Council and the Commission on the Realisation by Stages of Economic and Monetary Union in the Community' (The Werner Report), Luxemburg.

4. The Monetarists wanted, among other things, stabilization and an early fixing of exchange rates, the provision of generous credits for Member States facing BOP problems, control of capital movements and little supranationality. In contrast, the Economists did not want to fix exchange rates until the participating countries had reached a 'similar level of economic development' (this was never clearly explained). They wanted an early freeing of capital movements, the provision of modest credits for countries facing BOP problems and a high degree of supranationality. Surprisingly, both schools of thought were in broad agreement over fiscal integration.

4. The Record of the Single European Market

The origins of the Single European Market (SEM) were described in the introduction to this book. As was then discussed, the implementation of the SEM with the goal (but not obligatory) of 31 December 1992 is, in reality, simply a final implementation of the Treaty of Rome. This, then, involves the four freedoms: movement of goods, movement of people, movement of capital and establishment of services. In this chapter, I plan to examine the progress made to date in the four areas, the consequences thereof and the work still outstanding.

THE FREE MOVEMENT OF GOODS

In principle, the EC's achievement of the customs union meant that tariff barriers between the EC Member States – and the EFTA countries[1] – had been removed. However, among the non-tariff barriers, two major obstacles remained: taxation and standards.

Taxation

The acceptance of the value added tax (VAT) by all EC Member States as a common type of sales tax was a major fiscal achievement. But, so long as the tax level for the same products is too great (a variation of six percentage points would be acceptable), it is necessary to use the 'destination' principle (i.e. tax is levied at the point of consumption). Ever since the 1960s, the Commission has desired to implement an 'origin' principle (i.e. tax is levied at the point of production) in order to remove fiscal frontiers. Nevertheless, in the famous compromise arrived at in the Council of Ministers in the summer of 1992, a standard minimum VAT rate of 15 per cent was accepted and it was agreed that there would be regular exchanges of fiscal information between major corporations (which are responsible for most of internal Community trade), finance ministries and the Commission. The destination principle will remain until 1996. A compromise, though less far reaching in nature, was agreed for excise duties. Unfortunately, although a blueprint for the introduction of a Community corporation tax, using the 'imputation' method, has been on the table since 1973, no agreement was reached. To date, ten Member States use the imputation method – which has an inbuilt credit mechanism for recipients of share interest payments for tax already paid.

Thus, for all intents and purposes, controls over the movement of goods between EC Member States should, by now, have disappeared. For physical reasons this has not occurred at airports whilst Britain, Denmark and Ireland in any case still want to maintain controls. Also, whatever happens, customs controls for goods coming in from third party countries will remain.

Standards

Standards probably constitute the most insidious and effective non-tariff barriers to trade. In the old EEC, it was necessary for producers to make products for a number of separate national markets inside the EC rather than for one large one. Consequently, the Commission has sought to make standards similar by using three methods:

(i) selective harmonization whereby exactly the same standards would be mandatory throughout the Community,

(ii) mutual recognition whereby Member States would recognize each others' standards for the same products, and,

(iii) the exchange of information.

What, then, has been the progress to date? Many directives (some mandatory, some requiring transposition into national legislation) and regulations have been passed. Where safety is the criterion, the Commission has tended to opt for outright harmonization. This has been particularly the case for chemicals and dangerous substances, toys, pharmaceuticals and foodstuffs (though not for labelling). In the case of motor cars (the whole vehicle), Community-type approval will become mandatory in 1996.

Unfortunately, whilst all this progress is laudable where safety is imperative, the tendency is now, as has been lamented by the new director of the European Committee on Standards,[2] for the EC Member States to accept each other's standards. This implies that producers must, in many cases, make different products for individual EC national markets. My own experience in this field is salutary. When I recently tried to use electrical equipment in Brussels which I had bought in Amsterdam, I found that the Belgian plugs and sockets differ from the Dutch ones!

THE FREE MOVEMENT OF PEOPLE

This is a complicated legal issue which mesmerizes most European citizens. Where work is concerned, nationals of EC Member States have, since 1968, been able to seek and take up work throughout the Community (except in the Civil Service), and, having worked for some time in one Member State, to take up permanent residence there. But, with the exception of the Irish and the Italians, Community citizens have not, in contrast with their American counterparts, been very mobile. One of the reasons (though not the only one) for this state of affairs has been the lack of mutual recognition of qualifications. Here, the Commission and the Council have been very active. With temporary exemptions until next year for doctors (medical) in Germany and financial agents in Denmark and Britain, we have for all intents and purposes achieved mutual recognition of qualifications. Nevertheless, the actual transposition of the relevant directives into national legislation is another matter. A number of countries are seriously behind with this process and this may force the Commission to take legal action against them.

The actual free movement of citizens is more problematic. Retirees and students may move between EC Member States with complete freedom. The Commission stipulated that there be no controls on persons as from this summer and at the airports as from next January. For physical reasons, this has not and is unlikely to materialize before the middle of next year. Furthermore, for cultural and social reasons in the case of Denmark, and out of fear of terrorists and drug addicts in the case of Britain and Ireland, these three countries state that they will retain migration controls. It looks as though yet another financial bonanza is in store for all those unproductive lawyers. Then there is the Schengen Group[3] of countries which should have complete freedom of movement of persons between themselves in 1994.

THE FREE MOVEMENT OF CAPITAL

In the bad old days whenever capital movements were freed, money tended to flow out of Britain, France and Italy, and into West Germany and Switzerland (which has never been an EC Member State). Since early in 1992 all EC Member States, except Greece, have freed capital movements between themselves. It is true that during the major currency upheavals in 1992–93 some Member States did, temporarily, re-introduce controls. Nevertheless, the present freedom, after so many decades of control, is a major achievement.

THE FREEDOM OF ESTABLISHMENT OF SERVICES

Services comprise mainly, though not exclusively, the liberal professions and financial services. As has just been explained, with some exceptions, doctors, dentists, lawyers and others may freely set up practice in all EC Member States. The achievements already made for the liberal professions could constitute only a small economic benefit for the Community whereas freedom of establishment for financial services could lead to important savings and a widening of choice for European citizens.

Financial services account for some 7 per cent of the GDP of the Community. The Cecchini Report revealed tremendous differences in the costs and prices of similar financial services (see Table 4.1). This is, then, an area with the greatest potential savings. The main sectors concerned are banking, insurance and stockbroking. The opening up of these sectors involves agreement, among others, about reserve requirements, accounting and stockbroking practices and the implementation of the rules ensuring that priority in lending and the provision of credit facilities are not given to national and/or state organizations. In view of these preconditions, the progress made in the field of financial services is important. In banking, following the adoption of the Second Supervisory Directive at the end of 1989, a European banking passport allowing recognized banks in one EC Member State to set up branches in the other eleven, came into being at the beginning of 1993.

In the parallel area of insurance, major parts of the market had been opened up by May 1993, and a European insurance passport will be introduced in 1994, whilst the same type of passport will come into being for stockbroking in 1996.

PUBLIC PROCUREMENT

It is estimated that this most important area of economic activity accounts for approximately 15 per cent of the GDP of the Community. It has been, unlike the EFTA countries, an area most jealously protected by EC Member States for their own enterprises. In four critical areas – transport, energy, water and telecommunications – bidding for tenders for public procurement has been opened to all enterprises throughout the Community since 1991 in nine, and since 1993 in the remaining EC Member States. This means that, since the beginning of 1993, all public works contracts worth more than 5 million ECUs and all supplies worth more than 750,000 ECUs must be open to Community-wide competition.

Table 4.1 *Percentage differences in prices of standard financial products compared with the average of the four lowest national prices**

Standard service	B	D	E	F	I	L	N	UK
Banking services								
1. Consumer credit	-41	136	39	n.a.	121	-26	31	121
2. Credit cards	79	60	26	-30	89	-12	43	16
3. Mortgages	31	57	118	78	-4	n.a	-6	-20
4. Letters of credit	22	-10	59	-7	9	27	17	8
5. FX drafts	6	31	196	56	23	33	-46	16
6. Travellers cheques	35	-7	30	39	22	-7	33	-7
7. Commercial loans	-5	6	19	-7	9	6	43	46
Insurance services								
1. Life insurance	78	5	37	33	83	66	-9	-30
2. Home insurance	-16	3	-4	39	81	57	17	90
3. Motor insurance	30	15	100	9	148	77	-7	-17
4. Commercial fire and theft	-9	43	24	153	245	-15	-1	27
5. Public liability cover	13	47	60	117	77	9	-16	-7
Brokerage services								
1. Private equity	36	7	65	-13	-3	7	114	123
2. Private gilts	14	90	217	21	-63	27	161	36
3. Institutional equity	26	69	153	-5	47	68	26	-47
4. Institutional gilt	284	-4	60	57	92	-36	21	n.a

* The figures show the extent to which financial product prices, in each country, are above a low reference level. Each of these price differences implies a theoretical potential price fall from existing price levels to the low reference level.

Source: Cecchini Report

CONCRETE RESULTS

In concrete terms, to what degree has this combination of harmonization and opening up contributed to an increase in the GDP of the Community? According to EC statistics reproduced in Table 4.2, the contribution has not been great. There may be a number of reasons for this relatively disappointing result. First, it may be too early to measure the full effects of the SEM. Then, many of the directives have not been transposed into national legislation. Also, early evidence suggests that some countries are not stating the real value of public contracts thus keeping them just below the value where they would have to be opened up to Community-wide competition. Of at least equal importance is the fact that some most important areas of economic activity have not yet been opened up to Community-wide competition. It is to these areas which I will now turn.

Table 4.2 *Impact of '1992' on GDP and Employment*

	Impact on GDP (%)	*Impact on Employment (%)*
1988	1.2	0.3
1989	2.4	0.8
1990	3.4	1.3
1991	3.3	1.5
1992	3.4	1.5

Source: Commission of the European Communities

THE FUTURE

There are at least four important areas of economic activity which will have to be opened up in the coming years. The main areas are: Community-wide haulage/trucking, internal telecommunications markets, airline deregulation and internal energy markets.

The conception and implementation of a Community transport policy is laid down in the Treaty of Rome. Due to the visceral opposition of the German hauliers and truckers (the owners of the companies) who want German goods to be carried by German vehicles, the only progress to date has been a gradual increase in the number of Community-wide trucking passes issued each year. Fortunately, in 1993 the Council agreed to open up trucking by 1998.

The telecommunications markets have fabulous growth potential. As in the case of trucking, Germany, this time the Deutsche Bundespost, has wanted to keep the national monopoly for telecommunications. It was perhaps the combination of the trend toward privatization – with the notable example of Britain – and the necessity of making the EC competitive internationally that persuaded the Council to make a vital compromise. Thus, as from 1996, the market for cross-market telecommunications will be opened up whilst internal markets will be freed two years later. A five-year *derogation* or temporary exemption will be allowed for the economically least-developed EC countries.

Europeans frequently complain about the high European air fares when compared with the tariffs quoted in the United States for flying similar distances. Thus, it is no wonder that demands were made for a reduction in these jealously protected national monopolies and the bilateral fare agreements between national carriers. Thus, as from the beginning of this year, a partial deregulation has been in operation and airlines will be completely deregulated in April 1997.

Another field of great growth potential is energy. Here, no progress has been made in opening up the internal national markets. It is likely that we shall have to wait until the next century before we open up these markets.

In conclusion, I would say that whilst much progress has been made in implementing the SEM, much remains to be done. Apart from financial services, it is the opening up of big growth areas like the national telecommunications markets which will bring us the greatest economic benefits in future years. In all this, my greatest concern is for standardization where the trend is to recognize each other's standards rather than having common identical standards. This move, whilst not illegal, militates against the fundamental idea of a united SEM.

THE CULTURAL DIMENSION

Although the cultural dimension was never seen as being precisely a specific part of the SEM, the Community legislation of 1989, whereby 'Member States are to ensure, where practicable, and by appropriate means that broadcasters reserve a majority of their transmission time, excluding certain types of programme, for European works', could be interpreted as being a protectionist element of the SEM. In particular, EC Member States were allowed to interpret this directive (Council Directive of 3 October, 1989, OJEC L298, 17 October, 1989) in their own ways. Here, France has been particularly active and tries to ensure that 60 per cent of television programmes are European or purely French in origin.

Personally, I would welcome the maximum amount of cultural co-operation between European countries but doubt whether the 1989 legislation is the most practical way to achieve this. I do understand French concern about the invasion of Europe by American films and their desire to protect their film industry, still the most important one in Europe. Equally, I understand France's desire, which is shared by some of her EC partners, to keep cultural matters out of the current GATT Uruguay Round of multilateral trade negotiations. If the Community succeeds in this, it would be stategically wise to launch more national and European-financed trans-national film making projects as well as other European cultural co-operation plans.[4] In the meantime, more financing should be organized to promote these ventures throughout Europe as well as events like the annual Théâtre de L'Europe in Paris and the Edinburgh International Festival. In the same field and at an immediate and practical level, in June this year, the Council of Ministers accepted a four-year 228 million ECU plan to promote wide-screen television services throughout the Community. The original sum, requested by France and the Netherlands, had been 850 million ECUs.

NOTES

1. When Britain and Denmark joined the EEC in 1972 (the transition period started the following year), a reciprocal free trade agreement was signed between the EEC and EFTA countries. The coming into being of the European Economic Area between the two sides

(except Switzerland) will extend most of the tenets of the SEM to the EFTA countries.

2. The current development in standardization of EC Member States recognizing each other's standards has been bitterly criticized by Mr. Jacques Repussard, the new Secretary-General of the CEN, the European Committee for Standardization, in April last year, when he spoke of a 'rampant re-nationalization' of standardization procedures. Furthermore, he strongly rejected the Commission's call for the creation of a European Standards Institute and a Community logo, pointing out that his own institution, plus the CENELEC for the electronics sector and the ETSI for telecommunications, worked very well. Also, in June, the CEN concluded an agreement with the ISO, the International Standardization Organization, aiming at authorizing the presence of ISO observers in CEN committees and vice versa. To the author, this will be an important international development which will certainly be to the benefit of the Community and the United States.

    At an immediate practical safety level, according to the aims of the Commission, the CEN was expected, by the end of last year, to have set 4,500 standards, mainly in the areas of safety, for example, some 700 in the fields of construction, food and machine safety.

    Returning to his fierce denunciation of the EC Directive based on mutual recognition, Jacques Repussard pointed out that this (in my opinion) misnamed 'new approach' only contained general provisions and that surprisingly 'it was intended that the details would be worked out by private European standardization bodies.' The unbelievable finale to this saga is that the national public authorities (correctly) will not let these bodies take over responsibility for these duties! Hence, lawyers are, among other national experts, being called in to 'interpret' this directive. Where safety is involved, I am certainly of the opinion that the Community must have common standards. Certainly, the Commission's call, also made in April 1992, for common regulations and procedures for navigability and the implementation of 'Joint Airworthiness Requirements or JAR's' by mid-1993 are desirable and would give the Community a strong negotiating card *vis-à-vis* the United States.

    Although I have always stressed that we would not have an internal SEM like the internal market of the United States on 1 January 1993, whereby most spare parts would be interchangeable and all equipment will be able to be used throughout the European Economic Area (EEA) (thus depriving us from benefiting from economies of scale and long production runs on a European-wide stage), there are sectors where the adoption of common safety standards will lead to the creation of a real SEM. Probably the most important of these is the pharmaceutical sector. When, in April 1992, the Council adopted four important directives in medicine, they did, in effect, pave the way for the creation of a SEM in pharmaceuticals. These directives concerned (i) the wholesale distribution of medicinal products for human use, (ii) the classification with regard to supply of medicinal products for human use, (iii) the labelling and information on medicinal products for human use, and, (iv) the advertising of medicinal products for human use.

    Complementing these four very important directives, the Commission also submitted four proposals to the Council for the future system of authorization of medicines for human and veterinary use in Europe. The Commission also proposed the creation of a European agency for the evaluation of medicines.

    Finally, it is correct to say that we do (except where labelling is concerned) now have a SEM for pharmaceuticals.

3. The Schengen Group comprises all the EC Member States except Britain, Denmark and Ireland.

4. In 1988, the Commission requested the very modest sum of 5.5 million ECUs to finance its media programme. In view of the five major projects being prepared at the time (two for distribution, two on production and one on funding), this sum was clearly too low.

5. The Treaty on European Union: Realities and Myths

Too much has already been written about this wearisome and misleading Treaty on European Union (popularly known as the Maastricht Treaty). Writing about this Treaty in 1992,[1] I tried to remove misleading views about it as being a blueprint for a future United States of Europe which might be compared with the Constitution of the United States. Thus, I said:

> At a more elevated level, some observers had, wrongly, tried to compare the meeting of Community leaders in December, 1991, with the series of meetings of the Federal Convention, held in Philadelphia in 1787, by the Founding Fathers of the United States. Alas, alas, no comparison could have been further from the truth. At best, with few exceptions, the European leaders are technocrats (when we are lucky!) and/or party apparatchiks, dressed in their uniform undertakers' suits, lacking in vision and about as stimulating as rice pudding! Usually, they are engaged in horse-trading of the basest political kind and are not an inspiring bunch. Perhaps, wisely, there is, with occasional exceptions, no grand design for the future of Europe on the side of the Europeans. Consequently, those of us who do want a greater degree of cooperation in Europe do occasionally get a pleasant surprise, because, usually either unintentionally – or through some compromise, Europe does take a giant leap into the future. Nevertheless, at no time has a meeting of European leaders had as its mandate and mission the drawing up of a constitution for a United States of Europe.
>
> It is clear that Philadelphia fell into a completely different category than any of the afore-mentioned European meetings. First, the delegates were there for a special and specific purpose – the drawing up of a federal constitution for the nascent United States of America. Then, for the most part, they were highly educated persons – in some cases, they were intellectuals and/or enlightened universalists (one observer even talked of

demi-gods!). Finally, they were in Philadelphia for an indeterminate period of time – not for a few days! Hence, they had the time to create a constitution, which, together with subsequent amendments, serves the United States until this present day. Thus, the difference between the two sets of meetings could not be more glaring. Where then, are we at the institutional level, at this moment in time?

On the side of the United States, foreign governments deal directly with the Administration in the persons of the President himself, his ministers or immediate subordinates. The President must, however, seek the approval of Congress on a number of important issues – notably where trade and multilateral trade negotiations are concerned.

On the side of the Community, power is shared between institutions and countries. Regarding the latter, despite some of the aims laid down in the Treaty on European Union, individual Member States still maintain their independence in the fields of defence, foreign affairs, research and development, cultural affairs, capital investment flows, and, with the exception of money transferred to the European Development Fund, transfers of development aid to other countries. Furthermore, in the future, even if the Community does create an EMU with a European Central Bank, they will still be able to take part in bi-lateral monetary negotiations with other countries and institutions. The Member States, then, do still guard quite a degree of sovereignty.

Turning to the Community institutions themselves, the Treaty has given extended powers of consultation and delay to the European Parliament, but, if we exclude the European Court of Justice, the Court of Auditors and the Committee of Permanent Representatives, the two most powerful bodies are the Council of Ministers and the Commission. Although the Council must increasingly consult and co-operate with the Commission and the Parliament, it still wields considerable decision-making powers. Also, although more decisions are now taken on the basis of weighted majority voting, unanimity is still required for the taking of decisions in the following areas: fiscal and monetary policies, changes in the Treaty, social policy where labour law and/or finances are involved, and the admission of new members – though the last one with the approval of the Parliament by an absolute majority of all the registered members. It is, however, the Commission which is responsible for initiating legislation and for the daily management of Community agricultural, competition and industrial, regional, social and trade policies, and which manages (with the co-operation of the Central Banks of the Member States and the Bank for International Settlements) the EMS. It is also the Commission which negotiates on behalf of the Community in multinational trade negotiations. Consequently, at the much-heralded and subsequently disappointing summit between the two sides, held in Washington, D.C., on 22nd April, last year, the crucial meeting took place between President George Bush of the United States and President Jacques

Delors of the Commission of the European Community.

At a general international level, however, it is the Community's individual Member States – and not the European Community – which are members of the Council of Europe (not to be confused with the EC Council of Ministers), Western European Union (WEU), NATO, the OECD, GATT, the IMF and the World Bank – to give just the most important examples.

All these facts do give cause for considerable reflection when attempting to judge the feasibility of the Community's attempts to formulate a common foreign policy and common defence. Also, it is absolutely necessary to take into account the international political complexion of prospective candidates for Community membership.

(Coffey, 1993)

This Treaty, if and when it is ratified by all the twelve EC Member States (and the ratification process has been another story!), will replace certain parts of the Treaty of Rome and supersede the Single European Act. But, apart from the bribery and lack of information (except in the case of Denmark and the partial exception of France) which have cloaked the ratification process, the grave disquiet expressed about this Treaty by many observers as well as myself lies in the fact that it is a hotchpotch, a rushed job. The truth of the matter is that the Dutch tried to push through a blueprint for a European Federation, which received support only from Belgium and was thrown out of the window into the nearest canal (for once, Britain was not alone!) by the other ten Member States. Consequently, the necessity arose of hurriedly putting together a replacement treaty. Thus, recourse was had to a discussion paper presented by Luxemburg in June 1991. The result is an unbalanced Treaty in which a detailed timetable (an erroneous act as I wrote in the *Financial Times*[2] in 1992) is laid down only for the economic and monetary union (EMU).

A closer examination of Title I, the Common Provisions of the Treaty (reproduced at the end of this chapter), clearly shows that most of its contents are simply objectives. This is particularly the case concerning 'the implementation of common foreign and security policy including the eventual framing of a common defence policy, which might in time lead to common defence'.

Another objective is the introduction of a 'citizenship of the Union'

– whatever that may mean. In contrast, on the following line, 'to develop close co-operation on justice and home affairs', whilst the objective is fairly innocuous, it is interesting (as we shall see in Chapter 13) to note that discreet but effective co-operation in these fields is quite advanced between the relevant ministries and 'committees' of the Member States.

Although the Treaty is seen as a move towards greater integration and an 'even closer union among the peoples of Europe, in which decisions are taken as closely as possible to the citizen', most people haven't got the vaguest notion about what is going on. In fact, even Douglas Hurd, when he was putting his signature to the Treaty on 7 February 1992, said that he did not know what he was signing! Personally, I have the impression that the other ministers were equally in the dark about the whole business.

THE TREATY IN GREATER IN DETAIL

The preamble of the Treaty which sets down the main aims of the Treaty is reproduced on subsequent pages. However, as I have already mentioned, it is the chapter on the future economic and monetary union (EMU) where the Treaty is most generous in its details. In that chapter, it appears that the European Monetary Institute (EMI) which was created in January 1994 with the role of writing the constitution for a future European Central Bank will have much potential power. In contrast, with the exception of the annex on public debt obligations, the Treaty is frighteningly sparse concerning fiscal integration.

Task of the European Central Bank

In Article 105A of the Treaty, the ECB is empowered with the 'exclusive right to authorize the issue of bank notes within the Community'. However, interestingly enough both the ECB and the national central banks share the right to issue these notes. But it is the ECB which shall have the exclusive right to determine the volume of such notes, which, incidentally, will alone have the status of legal tender in the Community.

The sharing of tasks between the future ECB and the existing national central banks is underlined by the fact that they will, together, make up the European System of Central Banks (ESCB), which, in turn, shall be governed by the Governing Council and the Executive Board. According to Article 107 of the Treaty, both the future ECB and the existing national central banks are expected to be totally independent of the Community and the governments of the Member States! This implies a change in the status of some of the present national central banks. In the following article, Member States are expected to change their national legislation in order to be able to conform with this stipulation. *Voilà!* It is, however, the ECB alone that is empowered to issue regulations which will be binding on the whole Community. But, in Article 109, it is the Council, which, acting unanimously, has the right to 'conclude formal arrangements on an exchange rate system for the ECU in relation to non-community currencies'. Hopefully, the implication here is that the ministers concerned will be those in charge of finance! In contrast, the Council only needs to act by a qualified majority to 'adopt, adjust or abandon the central rates of the ECU within the exchange rate system'. In both cases the Council is expected to consult with the ECB – though, not necessarily, to agree with it. It is quite clear that the ministers will have a tremendous degree of authority within the ESCB. In a number of other areas of exchange-rate policy and in relations with international institutions, they only need a qualified majority in order to arrive at their decisions. However, and perhaps surprisingly, acting within the EMU framework, 'Member States may negotiate in international bodies and conclude international agreements'.

Article 109A of the Treaty lays down the institutional provisions for the ECB. In contrast with the Federal Reserve Board of the United States, their terms of office are relatively short:

1.   The Governing Council of the ECB shall comprise the members of the Executive Board of the ECB and the Governors of the national central banks.

2.   (a) The Executive Board shall comprise the President, the Vice-President and four other members.

(b)   The President, the Vice-President and the other members of the Executive Board shall be appointed from among persons of recognized standing and professional experience in monetary or banking matters by common accord of the Governments of the Member States at the level of Heads of State or of Government, on a recommendation from the Council, after it has consulted the European Parliament and the Governing Council of the ECB.   Their term of office shall be eight years and shall not be renewable.   Only nationals of Member States may be members of the Executive Board.

Treaty on European Union, 1992

A body which will almost certainly have an important advisory role is the future Economic and Financial Committee to be created at the beginning of the third stage of the EMU. This body will replace the Monetary Committee, which will have been created in the second stage and which will have given advice to the European Monetary Institute (EMI) whose main role will be to create the ESCB, and which will have replaced the present Committee of the Governors of Central Banks and the embryonic European Monetary Co-operation Fund.

Institutional Considerations

Reference has already been made to the continuing predominant role played by the Council of Ministers. Here, the Committee of Permanent Representatives (the COREPER) will continue to play a crucial role. However, the moment the Treaty is ratified the twelve permanent representatives will be flanked and/or 'shadowed' by a high ranking official of the Foreign Ministry of each EC Member State to help with the preparation of an eventual common foreign policy. Since this is a new policy option the prerogative for its preparation lies with the Council and the Commission is, to all intents and purposes, left out in the cold. This is an interesting development.

To me personally, the institutional development of great potential is the official place (for the first time) and recognition given to the EC watchdog, the Court of Auditors, as an official Community organ. In turn, the work of the Court should be given much more extensive publicity than is presently the case.

In a rather unsatisfactory and inadequate manner the expression 'subsidiarity' is mentioned in Article 3B. Here, the EC seems, though without any real explanation, to limit its powers: 'any action by the Community shall not go beyond what is necessary to achieve the objectives of the Treaty'. Does this mean that the long-term aim of the Community is to create a European type of Switzerland where the communes and regions (and in the case of the EC, the nation states) will keep substantial political powers and only delegate the nationally and internationally most necessary ones to the centre? The afore-mentioned development in the area of a common foreign policy would seem to support this trend.

A modest move in the direction of grass roots political representation is Article 8b whereby 'every citizen of the Union residing in a Member State of which he is not a national shall have the right to vote and to stand as a candidate at municipal elections in the Member State in which he resides, under the same conditions as the nationals of that State'. This potentially important political move has still to be voted on, unanimously, in the Council of Ministers before the end of 1994. We shall see.

Similarly, the right of petition by citizens of the Union to the European Parliament, via a parliamentary ombudsman, is a positive democratic development which is offset by the remoteness of this body. It is for this reason that, in the next chapter, I support Alan Sked's proposal that the Parliament should be composed of representatives of the national parliaments. This is particularly desirable in view of the increased consulting powers of this body – particularly where finance and the admission of new members are concerned.

At the institutional level, however, my greatest concern is for the role of the six-month Presidency of the Council of Ministers in the field of the common foreign and security policy. Thus, in Article J5, 1, of the Treaty, it is laid down that, 'the Presidency shall represent the Union in matters coming within the common foreign and security policy'. What happens, for example, if there are major upheavals in the Balkans during the Greek Presidency in the first six months of 1994? Will we see a repetition of the Yugoslav crisis under the presidency of Luxemburg and the Netherlands?

The Treaty, whilst allowing membership of existing alliances like NATO and WEU as well as bilateral agreements to continue as before, does not make adequate provisions for a future beset with dangers. I shall therefore attempt to remedy this dangerous oversight in the next chapter.

Protocol on Social Policy

Much has been written about this protocol, which, in principle, simply repeats the 1989 Social Charter which was accepted by all EC Member States except Britain. This Charter and the more recent Commission proposal for an 'equitable wage' have important economic implications for the Community. Consequently, I decided to examine these questions in a separate chapter on the Social Policy Issue (Chapter 12). Both of these important documents are reproduced in full at the end of this book.

Final Observations Concerning the Treaty

The Treaty on European Union is a rushed and hotchpotch job. It replaces parts of the Treaty of Rome and supersedes the Single European Act. It reaffirms the predominant role of the Council of Ministers whilst giving more power to the European Parliament. In the case of the latter, an ombudsman will be appointed to which citizens will have access. Also, a Conference of the Parliaments is called for.

Rightfully, the Court of Auditors is confirmed as a Community organ. In another vein, a Committee of the Regions is created. Will this committee lead to tensions with the governments of the Member States?

The long-run potential of the Treaty could be in the aim of a common foreign and security policy – eventually leading to common defence. Equally, however, this could lead nowhere.

The explanation of Community citizenship is dismissed in a few lines whilst the Member States are left to decide who is a national of their states. We shall return to this point later in the book. In a parallel field, a fairly innocuous chapter on police co-operation is being put into effect with a vengeance. Thus, instead of creating a 'Fortress Europe' for goods as the Americans feared some five years ago, we seem to be creating a human 'Fortress Europe'. As a sop, we have a Declaration on the Right of Access to Information which is neither here nor there.

Too much, far too much in fact, is said about the economic and monetary union, the European Monetary Institute and monetary policy. Astonishingly, apart from the protocol on public budgetary policy there is little or nothing about fiscal harmonization and/or integration. In contrast, the social policy chapter could be a contradiction to that on monetary policy should it lead to a common minimum European wage.

Finally, considering the uproar it has caused among European citizens, this Treaty is an inadequate document. It does, however, in an unbalanced fashion, lead to more European integration – without much accountability. Also, the fact that it must be accepted by all new EC Member States will make it more difficult for some European countries to join the Community in future.

NOTES

1. Peter Coffey, 1993, *EC and the United States*, London: Pinter Publishers.
2. Letter to the *Financial Times*, 28 July 1992.

Oversight on precise Emu date
From Peter Coffey

Sir, An oversight appears with alarming frequency in reports and articles in your own and other newspapers and magazines with regard to the final stage of European Economic and Monetary Union (Emu).

One frequently reads that, according to the Treaty on European Union, which was signed on February 7, 1992, that the third and final stage of Emu will begin no later than 1999.

However, if we examine article 109j, sections 3 to 5 (inclusive) of the treaty, we read that it is only if the date for the beginning of the final phase has not been agreed upon by the end of 1997 that it shall start on January 1, 1999.

The ministers could, though, decide on July 1, 2015, for example. Certainly, if as present, only two countries, France and Luxemburg, fulfilled the strict criteria for economic conveyance and budgeting deficits – as laid down in the relevant protocols – there would be little point in going on to the final stage at any time this century.

There is unfortunately already a precedent for setting down dates for an Emu. In 1970, the six founder member states of the European Economic Community accepted the second and definitive Werner report, which aimed at creating a full European monetary union by 1980! Alas, we are all too painfully aware of what happened to that attempt.

3. It should be noted that in order to become legal, this Treaty must be ratified by the parliaments of, or in a referendum in, the twelve EC Member States. At the time of writing, it had been ratified by 11 countries and was still before the German constitutional court as well as facing legal opposition in Britain. Britain has since ratified the Treaty.

APPENDIX TO CHAPTER FIVE: TREATY ON EUROPEAN UNION

Title 1:   Common Provisions

Article A

By this Treaty, the High Contracting Parties establish among themselves a European Union, hereinafter called 'the Union'. This Treaty marks a new stage in the process of creating an ever closer union among the peoples of Europe, in which decisions are taken as closely as possible to the citizen.

The Union shall be founded on the European Communities, supplemented by the policies and forms of co-operation established by this Treaty. Its task shall be to organize, in a manner demonstrating consistency and solidarity, relations between the Member States and between their peoples.

Article B

The Union shall set itself the following objectives:

to promote economic and social progress which is balanced and sustainable, in particular through the creation of an area without internal frontiers, through the strengthening of economic and social cohesion and through the establishment of economic and monetary union, ultimately including a single currency in accordance with the provisions of this Treaty;

to assert its identity on the international scene, in particular through the implementation of a common foreign and security policy including the eventual framing of a common defence policy, which might in time lead to a common defence;

to strengthen the protection of the rights and interests of the nationals of its Member States through the introduction of a citizenship of the Union;

to develop close co-operation on justice and home affairs;

to maintain in full the 'acquis communautaire' and build on it with a view to considering, through the procedure referred to in Article N(2), to what extent the policies and forms of co-operation introduced by this Treaty may need to be revised with the aim of ensuring the effectiveness of the mechanisms and the institutions of the Community.

The objectives of the Union shall be achieved as provided in this Treaty and in accordance with the conditions and the timetable set out therein while respecting the principle of subsidiarity as defined in Article 3b of the Treaty establishing the European Community.

Article C
The Union shall be served by a single institutional framework which shall ensure the consistency and the continuity of the activities carried out in order to attain its objectives while respecting and building upon the 'acquis communautaire'.

The Union shall in particular ensure the consistency of its external activities as a whole in the context of its external relations, security, economic and development policies. The Council and the Commission shall be responsible for ensuring such consistency. They shall ensure the implementation of these policies, each in accordance with its respective powers.

Article D
The European Council shall provide the Union with the necessary impetus for its development and shall define the general guidelines thereof.

The European Council shall bring together the Heads of State or of Government of the Member States and the President of the Commission.

They shall be assisted by the Ministers for Foreign Affairs of the Member States and by a Member of the Commission. The European Council shall meet at least twice a year, under the chairmanship of the Head of State or Government of the Member State which holds the Presidency of the Council.
The European Council shall submit to the European Parliament a report after each of its meetings and a yearly written report on the progress achieved by the Union.

Article E

The European Parliament, the Council, the Commission and the Court of Justice shall excercise their powers under the conditions and for the purposes provided for, on the one hand, by the provisions of the Treaties establishing the European Communities and of the subsequent Treaties and Acts modifying and supplementing them and, on the other hand, by the other provisions of this Treaty.

Article F

1. The Union shall respect the national identities of its Member States, whose systems of government are founded on the principles of democracy.

2. The Union shall respect fundamental rights, as guaranteed by the European Convention for the Protection of Human Rights and Fundamental Freedoms signed in Rome on 4 November 1950 and as they result from the constitutional traditions common to the Member States, as general principles of Community law.

3. The Union shall provide itself with the means necessary to attain its objective and carry through its policies.

Europe, Documents No. 1759/60 (February 1992)

6. The European Institutions: More or Less Democracy?

On 15 July 1993, the *Financial Times* reported that the Belgian Presidency of the EC Council of Ministers proposed the creation by the EC foreign ministers of a committee of 'wise men' who would look at the 'streamlining' of institutions in an enlarged European Community. This is clearly a proposal with important implications to which we shall return later in this chapter. But, first, what are these institutions, to what degree, if at all, are they accountable to EC citizens and how far should they be reformed in future?

If we put on one side for a moment the three important institutions: the Committee of Permanent Representatives (COREPER), the Court of Justice and the Court of Auditors, we are left with the Commission, the Council of Ministers and the Parliament. Unfortunately, these organizations do not behave in the same way as one would expect them to act in a Western parliamentary democracy.

THE COMMISSION

It is the Commission which initiates legislation. According to Jean de la Guérivière in his wonderful book, *Voyage À L'Intérieur De L'Eurocratie,*[1] there are currently about 25,000 Eurocrats in Brussels, 14,533 of whom are in the Commission. Hence, despite all the criticism about this institution, its numbers are those of a ministry in a large country like Britain. However, although it probably houses the biggest concentration of educated people in any international institution, there are not enough experts! Furthermore, whilst the Belgians and Italians tend to be grossly over-represented,[2] the British and Danes tend to be under-represented – though the nationals of the latter two countries score most highly in the entrance tests. In the upper echelons, the quality of the British and French Eurocrats tends to be very good indeed whilst Germany seems to send civil servants of more mediocre quality who do not reflect the importance of that country.

At the top of the Commission are 17 Commissioners – one for each small and two for each large Member State. These personalities, whatever their failings, can only be dismissed *en bloc* by the European Parliament. In reality, therefore, we can say that the Commission is not really responsible to anyone. Furthermore, it has the responsibility for managing the agricultural, competition and industrial, social, regional and trade policies of the Community. It can take institutions, business corporations and Member States to court if they persist in infringing the Treaty of Rome and subsequent legislation. Clearly, the Commission occupies a unique place among national and international institutions. However, unlike a civil service in any country in Western Europe, it does not assist and advise the ministers – but initiates the legislation! Thus, if the Community should wish to become just a simple confederation of states, the role of the Commission would have to be radically changed.

THE COUNCIL OF MINISTERS

Despite the legislative role of initiator enjoyed by the Commission and despite the greater degree of consultation which the ministers must enter into with the European Parliament, the Council of Ministers is the Community's decision-making body. Although it is responsible to the governments of the EC Member States and in this way to the national parliaments, it has only a consultative responsibility to the European Parliament since, unlike in other Western parliamentary democracies, it did not originate in that body. Furthermore, although the use of weighted majority voting (though a minimum eight Member States must vote on any issue) in the decision-taking process has increased over time, the rule of unanimity still holds good for the following: fiscal policies, monetary policies, social policies where finance (e.g. wages and salaries) is concerned, changes in the Treaties and the admittance of new members. Furthermore, where a Member State feels that its vital national interests are at stake it can threaten to use its right of veto – based on the Luxemburg Compromise of 1966.

The governments of Member States are able to greatly influence the choice of policies about which action should be taken, should they desire, when they assume the six-monthly rotating presidency of the Council which culminates in the twice-yearly European Summit. The drawback with such a system is that if a major international crisis blows up, it is difficult for the Community to act swiftly and energetically when the presidency is occupied by a small Member State. Such was the problem when the Yugoslav crisis exploded during the presidencies of Luxemburg and the Netherlands. In an attempt to partly remedy this situation, the Council has instituted the Troika System whereby major international issues will be dealt with by the present, preceding and the next immediate presidents of the Council. Still, despite this progress, this is not a really satisfactory state of affairs. We shall return to this problem later in this chapter.

It is the relatively unknown but immensely powerful Committee of Permanent Representatives (COREPER) which prepares the Council meetings and deputizes for the Ministers when they are not in Brussels.

THE EUROPEAN PARLIAMENT

The European Parliament is not, despite all the statements to the contrary, just a talking shop. It is a directly elected body, which, over the years, has gradually increased its powers. Thus, it can hold up approval of the Community budget and delay other legislation. Its power over the budget has considerable potential since both the Council and the Commission must reach a compromise, each year, on this matter with the Parliament. Unfortunately, however, ministers and governments do not emanate from this body – and that is its major drawback.

Another important problem faced by the Parliament is the disquieting and hilarious question of its permanent seat. Like nomads, with hundreds of trucks filled with documents, they move between

Strasburg, Luxemburg and Brussels. In fact, about 15 per cent of its budget is used for moving expenses. The French say that there was a Treaty agreement whereby the permanent seat should be in Strasburg. 'Nonsense!' retorts Emanuele Gazzo, Vice-President of the daily bulletin *Europe*. According to Mr. Gazzo, the Parliament first met in Strasburg because the building of the Council of Europe was, at that time, the most suitable edifice for its deliberations. It still rents the Council of Europe building (the new one) and has also purloined the Council's logo – the circle of gold stars against a blue background.

The members of the Parliament have voted to have its permanent seat in Brussels, where, incidentally, its committees meet. To this, the French Government has cried 'Illegal!'. However, discreetly, a Belgian group has just constructed a building in Brussels which can be used by the Parliament. We shall return to this later in this chapter.

THE COURT OF JUSTICE

The European Court of Justice, which meets in Luxemburg, is clearly a very important body, since, according to the French Conseil d'État and the British House of Lords, Community law takes precedence over national law. It is the European Court of Justice which interprets the laws of the Community and there is no appeal against its verdicts. It is, therefore, a very important body.

Although the judges and advocates-general of the Court are considered to be the legal *crème de la crème* of the EC Member States and although they are considered to be independent, the lack of a supreme court or council of appeal is extremely disquieting. Some reform would seem to be necessary here and this matter will be addressed at the end of this chapter.

THE COURT OF AUDITORS

This small overworked body of experts is probably the most European of all institutions. Its independence is guaranteed by the verification of its annual report by independent outside experts. Over the years it has increased its vigilance in the detection of fraud throughout the Community. Its work and annual reports should be made much more accessible to the citizens of the European Community.

AND DEMOCRACY?

From this brief examination of the main EC institutions it is clear that the democratic process is at best very thin. To this must be added the fact that in European countries where party lists are used in an electoral process of proportional representation, citizens have little or no access to their members of parliament. At least, in Britain, even Mrs. Thatcher held Saturday morning surgery (consultations) open to all her constituents. No, the European Community and its institutions are not particularly democratic. My only reservation here is that access to members of the European Commission is easy and that the Eurocrats are more open than most of their counterparts in national ministries. So, what should we do? Despite the flamboyant nature of his personality, the most sober and workable proposals for the reform of the Community's institutions have been made by Alan Sked. It is to these views that we shall now turn.

ALAN SKED'S PROPOSALS

Alan Sked, in his paper, 'A Proposal for European Union',[3] wants less government and favours a European Confederation. In this form of loose union he gives an important role to the European Parliament which he believes should become 'an assembly of representatives from national parliaments'. Personally, I find this to be a very sound proposal since it would give the Parliament real teeth enabling them to scrutinize the actions of the Council of Ministers. However, he wishes to extend the principle of the Luxemburg Compromise to the Parliament. Thus he proposes that:

If a majority of any national delegation objects to legislation proposed in the European Cabinet on the grounds that it undermines a vital national interest, and find their objections sustained by a majority of their national parliament, the proposed legislation, even if passed, will not be applicable to the country concerned.

Sked, 1990

He also wishes to give the following increased powers to the Parliament:

Scrutiny of the EC budget

Members of the European Parliament will have their powers strengthened by gaining the right to scrutinize the EC budget in detail and to amend or reject it by a majority vote. The European Parliament will not have the right to increase the EC budget without the consent of the EC Cabinet and Council.

In order to ensure that all member states contribute equitably, funds for the EC budget will derive from national quotas defined as an agreed proportion of national GDP. (There should therefore be no need for individual national rebates.)

It is proposed that, within the framework of the Single European Act, and with respect for national procedures, financial accountability be consolidated through the establishment, in each member state, of a visible European Community tax to raise the national contribution to the EC budget.

Legislation

All European legislation must be approved by a majority in the European Parliament.

The European Parliament will have the right to censure, by a majority vote, all members of the EC Cabinet.

Proposed changes to the Treaty of Union must be approved, in the first instance, by two-thirds of the European Parliament.

Sked, 1990

Alan Sked also proposes the creation of a real European Cabinet. Thus, he makes the following proposals:

The European Cabinet

The present Council of Ministers will be given increased status and responsibility by becoming a European Cabinet consisting of one national

minister from each member state.   The European Cabinet will be
permanently resident in Brussels, responsible for proposing and agreeing
European legislation, as well as the EC budget.

The European Cabinet will be responsible, in true parliamentary
tradition, to the European Parliament, and all EC Cabinet members will be
ex-officio members of the European Parliament.

Each member of the European Cabinet will also have cabinet status in
his domestic government (e.g. Secretary of State for Europe, instead of
Secretary of State for Scotland, Wales or Northern Ireland, to use the
United Kingdom as an example).

Each national Secretary of State for Europe will serve at the behest of
his national government and will be responsible for coordinating the work
of the European Cabinet with the work of the domestic cabinet.

The European Cabinet will distribute European portfolios amongst its
members under the direction of a rotating President who will make annual
'state of the Union' reports to the European Parliament.

The Presidency of the European Cabinet will rotate annually, from
amongst its members.

The voting procedure in the European Cabinet will rest upon the
principle of unanimity, except for areas specifically designated by the
European Council for majority voting.

The European Cabinet will sign trade and membership agreements on
behalf of the European Union provided these fall within the competence
of the Treaty and are approved by the European Parliament.

The European Cabinet will have the right to propose amendments to
the Treaty of Union.

                                                              Sked, 1990

However, according to Alan Sked, the present European Council
(Heads of Government) – with the rotating presidency for a period of
six months – will be one of the two supreme legislative organs.
Personally, I fear that there could be some conflict and confusion
between the European Cabinet and the European Council because
they would both have the right to propose European legislation.
Clearly, there would have to be a great deal of co-ordination between
the two bodies if problems are to be avoided.   Nevertheless, he
suggests the following roles for the European Council:

The European Council will continue to meet every six months as the
highest level coordinating body and will take responsibility for defence
and foreign policy of the European Union.

European political cooperation will be supervised by Heads of

Government and Foreign Ministers working with their own existing Secretariat.

The voting procedure of the European Council will rest upon the principle of unanimity save for areas specifically designated for majority voting, which will not include defence, foreign affairs and constitutional amendments.

The European Council will have the right, shared with the European Cabinet, to propose European legislation. Council initiatives will be put to the European Parliament for approval via the European Cabinet.

Proposed changes to the Treaty of Union, initiated in the first instance by the European Cabinet, and approved by a two-thirds majority in the European Parliament, will be referred to the European Council for acceptance. If adopted, amendments to the Treaty of Union will only come into force if passed with majority approval of two-thirds of all national parliaments.

Countries whose national parliaments reject these amendments will not be compelled to enter into new constitutional arrangements.

The European Council will suspend member states found to be in breach of the Peace Protocol.

Sked, 1990

This last point would, to me, require much greater explanation and detail before it could possibly be accepted by EC Member States.

Despite the criticism directed at the Commission by members of the Bruges Group, Alan Sked does suggest that it keep many of its present responsibilities – except that of initiating and proposing legislation – which should be exercised by the European Cabinet and Council. He also proposes merging the present Commission, the Council Secretariat and the COREPER into one European Civil Service. Henceforth, then, he proposes the following roles for the revamped Commission:

a) To review legislative progress and to take member states to the European Court if they default on their obligations under the Treaty of Union.

b) The right to issue directives, to issue regulations, etc., once these have been approved by the European Cabinet.

c) The right to negotiate treaties and administer funds under the supervision of the European Cabinet.

The European Commission will cease to have any political role

> (unlike the present Commission), and will not, for example, function
> as a middle-man between the European Parliament and the European
> Cabinet. Given the increase in powers of the European Parliament,
> this will no longer be necessary or desirable.
>
> Sked, 1990

Turning to the present European Court of Justice, he sees the need
for a supreme court and evidently finds that the present institution
exhibits too much institutional self-interest:

> Europe needs a supreme court. Given the number of member states,
> the diversity of their legal traditions, and the vested interests which have to
> be confronted in breaking down barriers in Europe, a supreme court is
> indispensable for furthering economic unity. It must also provide a
> guarantee of civil rights in Europe and help maintain the peace between
> European states. Democracy in short depends upon the rule of law and
> which rule is law in Europe can only be decided in a European court.
>
> Today, on the other hand, the European Court of Justice has an
> institutional self-interest in extending the competence of EC institutions
> and law by adopting a teleogical interpretation of legislation. The Court
> has also tended to boost the powers of the present European Commission
> and to neglect the exercise of judicial restraint. In short, there is
> insufficient provision within the existing treaties to impose a doctrine of
> 'ultra vires' or to encourage the Court to adhere to a strict interpretation of
> European law. Finally, as presently constituted, the Court has no
> responsibility for guaranteeing civil rights.
>
> Sked, 1990

Consequently, he makes the following proposals for the reform of
the Court:

1) The European Court of Justice will ensure the legality of European
   legislation proposed by the European Cabinet.

2) The Court will ensure that the European Cabinet and European
   Commission do not act 'ultra vires'.

3) The Court will ensure that the Treaty of Union and all European
   legislation is strictly interpreted.

4) The Court will guarantee the maintenance of human rights in the
   Community by entrenching the European Convention of Human

Rights.

5) Member states failing to uphold human rights will be expelled from the Community on the initiative of the European Court.

Sked, 1990

Personally, I find his fifth proposal to be much, much too extreme and I cannot believe that it would ever be accepted. Also, there is a major oversight in his proposals – there is, it appears, no room for appeal. Thus, I would propose that a European Court of Appeal should be set up consisting of members of the upper houses of national parliaments of the EC Member States.

MY OWN PROPOSALS

With reservations I have already made, I do, in principle, accept Alan Sked's proposals – provided that our aim is the creation of a European Confederation or a European kind of Switzerland. Having said this, there is, with the impending enlargement of the Community, an immediate and urgent need to streamline the present institutions. Consequently, I would make the following proposals for reform:

1. Regarding the Commission, the present situation whereby each major Member State has two commissioners and each small one has one commissioner is already untenable. Thus, I propose that each large country have only one commissioner whilst each group of small countries, e.g. the Benelux and the Scandanavian countries, should also have one commissioner. Also, the Commission should no longer have the right to initiate and propose legislation.

2. Alan Sked's proposal for the election of representatives from the national parliaments to the European Parliament should be immediately implemented.

3. A kind of European Senate – consisting of representatives of the upper houses of EC Member States should also be created. This organ

would act as a European Supreme Court of Appeal.

4. In the immediate future, the present Council of Ministers should remain until such time as a permanent European Cabinet can be set up. Its deliberations should, however, be much less secretive than is presently the case. Furthermore, in view of the observations I have made earlier in this chapter, I doubt the wisdom of maintaining the rotating presidency.

5. Regarding the permanent location of the principal Community organs, clearly the present nomadic nature of the European Parliament is a costly absurdity. Logically, the Council, the Parliament and the Commission should all be situated in Brussels.

The proposals I have just made are, I believe, practical proposals which, hopefully, will make the Community and its organs more workable in the immediate future. In the longer run, with the reservations I have made, I believe Alan Sked's proposals to be extremely important and valid.

My conclusions are that we need much more democracy in the European Community and we should not be fobbed off by that bizarre expression, 'subsidiarity' – whatever that may mean. Rather, citizens should be able to see institutions actually working on their behalf and should have access to their members of parliament and ministers.

Although the members of the Commission are accessible, educated and helpful, they should not be burdened with the responsibility of initiating and proposing legislation. Furthermore, since too much of their budget is spent on translation and interpreting services, the use of French and English as the working languages should be extended and reinforced. With the resulting savings, the Commission could engage more sorely needed experts, for example, in the control of mergers between companies, the control of fraud and in relations with individual Third World countries – all very important activities for which the Commission just does not have enough experts.

In conclusion, however, citizens need to be more clearly associated with the Community and its institutions and the only way to achieve this aim is by having more democratic contact and control and a much greater degree of visibility. For this reason, I would propose that the constitution of a future European Confederation should be the following main preamble of the European Convention on Human Rights which clearly lays down our basic rights as citizens of Europe:

> The following rights are covered by the collective guarantee of the Contracting Parties to the Convention: the right to life; the right to liberty and security of person; the right to the fair administration of justice [the right most frequently invoked before the organs of the Convention]; the right to respect for private and family life, home and correspondence; the right to freedom of thought, conscience and religion; the right to freedom of expression and opinion; freedom of assembly and association, including the right to form trade unions; the right to marry and found a family; the right of persons whose rights set forth in the Convention are violated to an effective remedy before a national authority, notwithstanding that the violation has been committed by persons acting in an official capacity; the right of property; the right to education, which is defined as follows: 'No person shall be denied the right to education. In the exercise of any functions which it assumes in relation to education and to teaching, the State shall respect the right of parents to ensure such education and teaching in conformity with their own religious and philosophical convictions'; an undertaking by States to hold free elections at reasonable intervals; prohibition of torture and of inhuman or degrading treatment or punishment; prohibition of retroactive criminal legislation; prohibition of discrimination on any ground in the enjoyment of the rights and freedoms set forth in the Convention.*

> * Four additional rights and freedoms not included in the Convention and the First Protocol are set out in Protocol No. 4: freedom from imprisonment for debt; freedom of movement and of the choice of one's residence; freedom of expulsion from, and the right to enter one's own country; prohibition of the collective expulsion of aliens.

> European Convention on Human Rights, 1959

NOTES

1. Jean de la Guérivière, 1992, *Voyage À L'Intérieur De L'Eurocratie*, Paris: Le Monde Editions.
2. According to David Gardner in his article, 'EC given food for thought over allocating plum jobs', *Financial Times*, 29 March 1993:

> '...of the 93,691 applicants for the 3,459 A-grade posts advertised by competition in

1986-1991, the Commission report shows the UK fielded only 4,983 and Denmark only 1,574, against 24,734 from host country Belgium, 18,529 from Italy and 10,333 from France'.
3. Alan Sked, 1990, 'A Proposal for a European Union', Bruges Group, London.

7. Enlargement and/or Greater Depth?

The following are the criteria which countries must fulfil if they wish to even consider becoming members of the European Community:

1. they must be European countries,
2. they must be multi-party parliamentary democracies,
3. they must be market-type economies, and
4. they must respect human rights.

Thus, apart from the actual geographical definition of Europe, these criteria are perfectly clear. Even regarding the question of geography, we do at least know that it means countries north of the Mediterranean because, when the King of Morocco sought EC membership for his country, the Commission replied, 'Your Majesty, we very much like your country but Morocco is not a European country' (my paraphrasing). On this geographical point, I would say that we are concerned with all the countries of Western and Eastern Europe, the Baltic States but not, in principle, the countries of the former Soviet Union – we shall, however, return to this point later in this chapter. Should we, then, deepen or enlarge the Community? Let us look at the arguments in favour of both cases.

DEEPENING THE COMMUNITY

Understandably, both President Mitterand and Chancellor Kohl would prefer to deepen the Community before taking on board new Members, and, provided that all 12 Member States do ratify the Treaty on European Union, they will have achieved their aim. Why should this be so? The ratification of this Treaty makes it harder for all but the most advanced European countries to become EC Members – and they must accept this document as well as the Treaty of Rome and the intervening *acquis communautaires*. The French and German Heads of Government, with their memories of both World Wars which nearly destroyed both their countries, wish to anchor Germany more firmly into the European family of nations. Personally, I feel that this has now been achieved and the case for widening the Community – with some reservations – becomes stronger.

WIDENING THE COMMUNITY

The four countries currently negotiating their membership of the Community, Austria, Finland, Norway and Sweden, all completely fulfill the four criteria for EC membership. They are all economically highly developed West European parliamentary democracies and they will make a net contribution to EC funds. They will, equally, bring problems with them as will any widening of the Community. With four new Member States, the decision-making process will become infernal if not impossible. As examined in the last chapter, there is the problem of the number of Commissioners – is each of the new Members going to receive the post of Commissioner? According to the Treaty of Rome, this must be so, hence the urgency of institutional reform. Then, there is the problem of the rights of veto in the Council of Ministers.

Another problem is that of neutrality. All the four new Member States, except Norway, are neutral. How does this square with the Treaty on European Union and its declared aim of common defence? Hitherto, Ireland's policy of neutrality did not cause any problems – but now there will be five neutral Members. Surely the way out of this dilemma would be a very flexible interpretation of the Treaty on European Union – or a policy of 'Europe à la carte'. I do not see any other solution to this problem.

THE FUTURE:
A FURTHER WIDENING OF THE COMMUNITY

Turkey's application for membership was rejected because the 'time was not yet ripe' – but that country will, as is its right,[1] certainly re-submit its application. What will be the reaction of Greece to this? Yet Turkey, as it develops much further economically, politically, and socially – and because of its strategic position – cannot be left out in the cold forever.

Then there are the countries of Eastern Europe and the Baltic States. Although relations with these countries will be examined in the next chapter, it should be noted that when the Community signed the association agreements with the Visegrad countries,[2] a protocol was attached whereby their eventual requests for EC membership would be examined with consideration.

Personally, I feel that we can, if we wish, have the best of both worlds – we can both widen and deepen the Community at the same time. Whilst we have a moral obligation to accept all European countries which desire and qualify for EC membership, there will inevitably be some countries, notably in the fields of economic, monetary and defence policies, which wish to integrate more swiftly than others. Nevertheless, if we want the widening of the Community to be really feasible, we have to first reform the institutions.

A consideration of much greater and more immediate importance – which I shall examine in greater detail later in this book – is that of defending, *militarily*, new EC Member States. As I shall explain later, there has hitherto been an understanding that the Community does defend the territorial integrity of its Member States. Clearly, this privilege must be extended to any countries which are eligible for membership. Thus, the situation of prospective Member States must give grounds for concern.

Among the prospective members, Turkey is the one which will cause the least problems. Like Britain and Greece, Turkey has always spent a large amount of its GDP on defence. Also, she is a loyal member of NATO. Among the other countries, Norway is a member of NATO and presents no problems. But, what about Austria, Finland, Sweden – and eventually, possibly Switzerland?

The possible future membership of the Baltic States and countries of Eastern Europe presents further problems. We could not possibly offer membership to these countries unless we are really intent on defending them *militarily*.   But this would necessitate enlisting the understanding of Russia.

NOTES

1. According to the Treaty of Ankara by which Turkey became an associate member of the EEC, she has the right to apply for full membership at the end of the transitional period. That period has long since expired. As from 1995 a customs union will exist between the EC and Turkey.
2. The Visegrad countries comprise Hungary, Poland and the Czech and Slovak Republics.

8. Policies for Eastern Europe

THE BACKGROUND

We were all surprised when it all happened, or were we? One person, at least, Hélène Carrère D'Encausse,[1] had forecast the collapse of the Soviet Empire in precise detail in 1978. But, what exactly was this system which collapsed, taking with it both the CMEA and the Warsaw Pact? We are talking about a system in which the means of production were owned by the State – although in some East European countries private property was allowed as well as small privately-owned enterprises such as restaurants and small shops. Regarding this latter development, Hungary had gone further than the other countries. Then, on top of this system of ownership, a State system of economic planning (very detailed indeed in the case of the Soviet Union) was imposed on these countries in which the fulfilment of quantitative norms rather than quality was the yardstick. Furthermore, subsidies and different artificial exchange rates to a large degree cut off these countries from the international trading system. Another economic phenomenon peculiar to these countries was their degree of self-sufficiency. They were trading, at the most, only 10 per cent of their GDP. Added to this was the fact that they were, with the notable exception of Hungary, trading heavily with CMEA countries. To crown all this was the dominant position of the former Soviet Union in this trading organization.

Even before the collapse of the Berlin Wall, some of these countries – led by Hungary – were trying to trade more with the West. However, they complained about Western trade barriers – notably the Community's CAP and the work of COCOM.[2] In reply, Western countries have complained about the poor quality of products coming from the countries of the former Soviet bloc and the impossibly low prices – which they qualify as being 'dumping'. Despite all these criticisms, at the time of the collapse of the Berlin Wall, the European Community had signed bilateral trade agreements with all East European countries, except Albania and East Germany,[3] and was in the process of negotiating an agreement with the former Soviet Union .[4]

Both culturally and politically the countries of Central and Eastern Europe had had a long history and differed considerably from each other. For example, the union of Poland and Lithuania had created the greatest Central European Roman Catholic State by the end of the seventeenth century – before disappearing for over a hundred years late in the eighteenth century. The Austro-Hungarian Empire, for all its major defects, created sophisticated administrative and educational systems which left an indelible mark on the countries concerned. These facts, plus profound cultural, ethnic and religious differences account, to a large degree, for some of the problems facing Eastern Europe today. Also, we should not forget that before World War II the former Czechoslovakia, shamelessly betrayed by Britain and France at Munich in 1938, was the only real fully multi-party democratic parliamentary system in Central and Eastern Europe (Here, I do not include all the Baltic States. Latvia did have an Italian-type fascist régime in 1939.)

Politically, despite the existence of the one-party state in most countries of Eastern Europe, there were differences among them. Thus, the intellectual atmosphere was much, much freer in Hungary and Poland. In contrast, Romania remained Stalinistic long after the death of Stalin – whilst a form of cultural genocide was imposed on the former Czechoslovakia after the invasion of the troops of the Warsaw Pact in 1968. Also, despite the idea of the one-party state, some countries still allowed small political parties to function, albeit mainly for purposes of window-dressing. Thus, when the Berlin Wall did come down, we were not faced with a completely homogeneous group of countries. So, what have we done so far and what should we do?

THE REACTION OF THE EUROPEAN COMMUNITY

At the cultural and educational levels the European Community was very quick off the mark in creating, in 1990, the TEMPUS Programme to finance partnership projects – mainly through the exchange of professors and students – between educational institutions in the EC and Eastern Europe. This has been a highly successful programme which is bringing on stream 234 new projects in the 1992–93 academic year.

At a more technical and business level, and involving 24 Western countries, the PHARE programme has been organized for businesses (notably to encourage private enterprise) in Eastern Europe. Similarly, the TACIS programme has been organized for the countries of the former Soviet Union.

But, apart from these programmes plus the provision of aid, both bilateral country to country or Community funded, and loans from institutions such as the European Bank for Reconstruction and Development (EBRD) and the European Investment Bank, the former CMEA countries are interested in trade. Here, the EC (also, the EFTA countries which have signed free trade agreements with the Visegrad countries) has signed association agreements with the Visegrad countries, Bulgaria and Romania. Basically, these agreements involve the immediate removal of quotas and the speedy removal of tariffs on the side of the EC. However, the concessions on so-called 'sensitive products', notably textiles, steel and agricultural products, are less generous. Alas, these are precisely the type of products for which the East and Central European countries have a comparative advantage. In contrast, the protocol on services satisfied the East and Central Europeans.

In reaction to the complaints made by these countries, at the beginning of May, the Commission proposed a package of reforms which were accepted, almost in their entirety, at the Copenhagen Summit the following month. According to the *Financial Times* of 1 and 2 May 1993, the main elements were as follows:

1. Removing all tariffs for industrial goods such as cars and chemicals by the end of 1994. This cuts an earlier five-year transition period to three years.

2. Reducing the period for phasing out tariffs in 'sensitive sectors' such as textiles and steel from five to four years. This means a cut of 20 per cent each year, with a 40 per cent reduction in the fourth year.

3. Increasing quotas and ceilings from 20 per cent to 25 per cent for sensitive goods – so-called because of the East Europeans' competitive advantage.

4. Advancing plans to increase exports of meat, fruit, dairy goods and vegetables from East European countries by 10 per cent annually for five years. The plan has been brought forward by six months to begin this July.

5. Moving from a quota-based system which sets rigid targets for imports into less restrictive 'ceilings'. This means East European exporters will not automatically face higher tariffs if they exceed their import targets, a senior EC official said.

Financial Times, 1993

Perhaps of greater interest are the 10-year co-operation agreements signed between the Community and the Baltic States and Albania in May, 1992. Whilst including a trade agreement (though textiles and clothing are included in a separate accord) with wide-reaching economic co-operation, they place particular emphasis on the importance of democratic principles and human rights as laid down in the Helsinki Final Act and Charter of Paris.

Trade between the two sides has increased and the EC surplus *vis-à-vis* these countries is declining. Yet, there is the feeling that not enough is being done, and, maybe, we are not applying the right policies, so, what should we do?

FUTURE POLICIES

At the outset I should stress that we Europeans, sitting comfortably in our homes in Western Europe, have a moral obligation to encourage and help our brothers and sisters in Eastern and Western Europe. For years, we called on them to overthrow Communism. Now that they have done this and the Russians have removed almost all their troops from these countries, it is up to us to help them. But, what exactly should we do, what should they do and which countries, if any, could possibly eventually apply for membership of the EC? First, however, I should say that I do not wish to include an examination of the former East Germany in this chapter since that is a specific case and trade between the two Germanies was treated by the Community as internal German trade.

As already mentioned, the countries of Eastern and Central Europe differ greatly from each other. Thus, at the outset of World War II, some countries, notably the former Czechoslovakia, Hungary, Poland and the Baltic States, did have flourishing market economies. Most of the other countries were more backward economically, whilst the former Soviet Union was already living in another world, economically speaking. Hence some countries still have memories of a capitalist system. Now, Poland has opted for a shock therapy approach of privatization and the Czech Republic and Hungary have adopted a slower but still determined policy of privatization. Personally, despite the relative success of the Polish experiment, I fear that we are trying to impose too quickly on countries of Eastern and Central Europe – as well as the former Soviet Union – a system of capitalism which we do not even have in Western Europe. What I mean by this is that, despite the recent moves in privatizing the economy in EC Member States, the State is still a major owner of the means of production, especially in France and Italy but also to some degree in Germany and elsewhere. What really matters is that we should encourage the former CMEA States to adopt a system of 'workable competition'. What I mean by this is that there should exist no legal barriers to the entry into an economy by new producers and purveyors of services and that there should exist competition between state enterprises. The actual percentage occupied by these countries in EC imports is very small indeed and we could certainly open up our markets further to increased imports from them. Where 'sensitive' products are concerned, the EC should provide financial help to producers on both sides of the former Iron Curtain either to move into technologically more sophisticated sectors of the economy and/or to modernize their existing factories.

More aid? Yes, but again, for specific projects. An endless number of projects are waiting for us: the environment, the transformation to civilian production of former military installations, transport, the communications infrastructure. All these require a mixture of financial aid and training but the programmes are in place and only need intensifying.

Apart from bilateral agreements between the countries of Eastern and Western Europe, it is equally important and necessary that the CMEA countries should not completely break the old trade links between them. What is needed is a system of smaller regional units which can trade together and also negotiate internationally from a position of strength. There are signs that this could happen. Thus, the Visegrad countries are considering the creation of a free trade area among themselves, whilst Russia, Belarus and the Ukraine have agreed to create an economic union. Recently, the Baltic States have signed an agreement creating a free trade area between themselves.

Politically, what will happen? Will democracy become firmly established in these countries, what should we do to help them and which, if any, of these countries will possibly qualify for EC membership? Certainly we are helping them by supporting their applications for membership, especially of the Council of Europe as well as other more international organizations. Above all, it is in the Council of Europe where they will learn democratic and parliamentary habits. At the time of writing, Hungary had become the latest member of this organization. What hopes are there for democracy? Professor Robert Farlow of the University of St. Thomas considers that the Czech Republic will make it. Then, probably Hungary and Poland. To this short list I would add the Baltic States. It is in this order that I would rank the order of possibility of these countries joining the European Community – sometime in the next century.

FOOTNOTE

In view of the upheavals which have surrounded the replacement of Jacques Attali by Jacques de Larosière as the head of the European Bank for Reconstruction and Development (EBRD), established in 1990 and based in London, and the impending changes in the management of this institution, I have decided not to examine its activities in any detail in this chapter. It should be noted however, that this bank, in which the EC has a majority holding, has capital of 10 billion ECUs – financed by a number of Eastern and Western countries, including the European Investment Bank (EIB). Its activities, which promote private enterprise, are undertaken in Eastern and Central European Countries as well as in the countries of the former Soviet Union.

NOTES

1. Hélène Carrère D'Encausse, 1978, *L'Empire Éclaté*, Paris: Flammarion.
2. The COCOM or Co-ordinating Committee on Multilateral Export Controls, with an office in Paris, consists of 17 countries: the NATO countries (except Iceland) plus Japan and Australia. Its role is to monitor exports of technological products which could be used in the production of military weapons.
3. It will be remembered that trade between the two Germanies was classified as internal German trade.
4. The reason why it had taken so long to reach agreement between the EC and the former USSR was that the Soviets had never wished to recognize the Community as a legal entity.

9. Present and Future Economic and Monetary Policies

The present European Community was, until recently, aptly named the European Economic Community (EEC), and, as was shown in the first chapter of this work, its aims were mainly economic in nature. Then, as was examined in Chapter 3, at the meeting of Heads of Government of the EEC Member States in the Hague at the end of 1969, it was agreed to create a full 'economic and monetary union' (EMU) – provided that 'the political will to do so exists'. The first manifestations of this agreement were the 'Snake in the Tunnel' and the 'Snake Arrangement' – neither of which were very successful. Their successor, the European Monetary System (EMS), was considered, until the upheavals of late summer and autumn 1992, to have been a success. But why should the Community, as early as 1969, have thought itself to be a good candidate for a full EMU? As was examined in Chapter 3, in several works,[1] I have suggested the following reasons for this decision. These countries had, by 1968, achieved most of the aims as laid down in the Treaty of Rome. Quite simply, ahead of time, the customs union had been achieved. Consequently, the economies of the Member States had become well integrated and they were conducting about half their trade among themselves. Then, there was the position of the Community's Common Agricultural Policy. The successful functioning of this policy depended upon stable (preferably fixed) exchange rates. At an international level the EEC had become the world's most important economic and trading bloc, endowed with the most important reserves of gold and convertible currencies. France had, for a number of years, considered that the Community should consequently be endowed with a 'common international monetary personality'. One of the best ways of demonstrating such a personality would be to create an EMU and a common currency.

The very fact that the EC Member States are 'open' or 'very open' economies – conducting 60 per cent of their trade with each other (see Table 9.1) – means that they will automatically demand each other's currencies.

Table 9.1 *Degree of 'openness' in national economies in 1991*
(as a percentage of GDP)

	Exports	*Imports*
Belgium	74.4	71.3
Denmark	35.8	29.9
Germany	33.7	27.8
Greece	20.7	30.1
Spain	17.1	20.2
France	22.7	22.4
Ireland	63.5	56.3
Italy	20.3	20.1
Luxemburg	97.8	101.4
Netherlands	56.4	50.7
Portugal	32.0	42.2
United Kingdom	23.8	24.2

Source: EC Commission

Unfortunately, herein lies the tension in the system. In the case of a country like Ireland, whose trade is divided between the United Kingdom and the other EC countries, then her currency will be pulled between the pound sterling and other currencies. In contrast, a country like the Netherlands, called an 'economic satellite of Germany' by a director of the Bundesbank, will logically link its currency with the Deutsche Mark. Of course, in an EMU there are other considerations as well as trade – economic policies must be co-ordinated. Thus, in the case of the EMS (which I have always seen as being the first stage of an EMU), four logical policy steps were accepted by active members of the Exchange Rate Mechanism (ERM). Thus, the responsibilities of the country concerned when the Divergence Indicator is reached *vis-à-vis* the ECU by its currency, are clearly laid down by the Resolution of the Council of Ministers of 5 December 1978. They are:

1. diversified intervention
2. monetary measures
3. drawing on credit facilities
4. external and domestic policy measures

In detail, these measures imply that when a participating country's currency comes under pressure on the exchange markets, that country – and the other countries whose currencies are concerned – will intervene on the markets in an attempt to remedy the situation. If this action fails, then the country concerned will raise or lower interest rates. Then, it may have recourse to the generous short and medium-term credits available under the EMS. Fourthly, if all these three sets of action are of no avail, then the country concerned will be obliged to take internal and external economic action – normally of a fiscal nature. Finally, if all this fails to improve the position of the currency which is under pressure, a swift and discreet exchange rate re-alignment may have to be operated. All in all, these are indeed major commitments which have been voluntarily accepted by these countries.

These were reinforced by the Nyborg/Basel Agreement of 1987 for economic and monetary policy co-ordination between EC Member States. Unfortunately, in 1992, participants in the ERM completely ignored the four aforementioned policy steps whilst there was little or no policy co-ordination. Despite this irresponsibility, there then came the stiff criteria for membership of an EMU – plus the nonsensically rigid time table in the Act on European Union – but that is another story.

But, in terms of action or inaction, what were the EC Member States doing in 1992? According to Peter Norman and Lionel Barber, writing in the *Financial Times* on 11 and 12 December 1992, the guilty person is Jean-Claude Trichet, who recently received a very important promotion by the French Government. They accuse Jean-Claude Trichet, Director of the French Treasury and Chairman of the EC Finance Ministers and Heads of Central Banks during the weekend of 12 September, of failing to organize a broad and orderly re-alignment of currencies – which apparently the Germans wanted, instead of which, following devastating speculation, both the British and Italian currencies left the EMS.

Equally, the Bundesbank is accused of a rigid adherence to monetary orthodoxy. Even more astounding is the revelation that during the weekend of 12 and 13 September, when it was evident that a re-alignment of currencies was inevitable, and when a devaluation of the Italian lira had, in fact, been decided upon by Italy, the Bundesbank failed to contact either the Bank of England or the British Government (the pound sterling was, like the Italian lira, under speculative pressure on the currency markets). Furthermore, the secretary of the EC Monetary Committee, Mr. Andreas Kees, whose job is to canvas the views of other Member States when one or more countries have decided upon a currency re-alignment, was, apparently, 'away boating'! Of equal disbelief was the reaction of the British officials. . . they were surprised! In fact, so surprised were the author's fellow countrymen that Whitehall apparently had to:

> mount a large-scale search operation to trace Sir Terry Burns, the permanent secretary to the Treasury. He was finally tracked down in Dulwich, a south London suburb, at a party celebrating a friend's 25th wedding anniversary. He learned the news on a mobile phone from Sir Nigel Wicks, the second permanent secretary, who, conscious of the recent security breaches on mobile phones, would only refer obliquely to a problem with 'our sick friend'. Mr. Lamont, who was at the last night of the Proms, was also only told of developments at a late stage.
>
> Although there was some concern that the lira devaluation could mean further volatility in the ERM ahead of France's referendum, there was no sense of imminent doom early on Sunday when Mr. Lamont met senior officials in the UK Treasury to discuss developments. By then, according to UK officials, it was known the Bundesbank would cut its Lombard rate by $1/4$ percentage points the next day and announce cuts of $1/2$ point in its

discount and money market rates.

When Sir Terry asked, as a matter of form, whether sterling would join in the realignment with a devaluation, the answer from the chancellor was 'No'.

Financial Times, 11 and 12 December, 1993

EC Economic Success and Failures

The fact that 60 per cent of EC trade is internal is, in itself, an important achievement – though I suspect part of this is due to that scandalous misallocation of economic resources – the Crazy (sorry!)... Common Agricultural Policy (CAP) – about which I shall say virtually nothing in this work. Apart from this achievement, and the laudable degree of success in implementing so much of the Single European Market (SEM), there have been considerable ups and downs in economic policy whilst today, with the partial exception of Britain, we find ourselves in a period of recession. This stagnation is not new – we experienced something similar – though less severe – in the period 1979–84. But this was followed by a time of economic expansion between 1985–90. Over this period, investment rose by 43 per cent and output by 14 per cent and unemployment declined. Apart from national economic and monetary policies, I find that there were two main reasons for this wonderful period of expansion. One was the anticipation of the SEM and the other was Portugal's and Spain's entry into the EEC which led to fabulous inflows of capital investment into those two countries. So, is the secret for future expansion to open up the SEM much further and to admit more and more members to the EC? Maybe, but we shall return to this question later in this work.

At the present time there is a world recession which seriously affects the Community but Alfonso Jozzo[2] believes (and I share his views) that one of the probable causes of past expansion and the present structural problems inside the EC has been the level of debt. Thus he writes:

> The size of the debt has been certainly inherited from the past and its origins vary from country to country. In the United Kingdom, during the course of the 80s, lax monetary policies and financial liberalization led to

a steep rise in private debt (households and non-financial enterprises) as a percentage of the national product (from 135% in 1980 to 265% in 1991, according to OECD data). In France the same ratio rose as high as 300% (from 184% in 1980) and was largely due to heavy corporate indebtedness. In other countries, unrestrained fiscal policies pushed government debt up to danger levels; in 1992 the ratio of public debt to domestic product in Italy reached 107% and looks set to continue its explosive growth; it is currently standing at 132% in Belgium and just 100% in Ireland.

The level of growth rate of debt stock highlights the problem of the scarcity of national savings which German unification, with the request for high domestic interest rates, and the consequent drain of capital from abroad have undoubtably magnified. The sequence of events in 1992 linked to the ratification process of the Treaty of Maastricht have only served to point out the latent problem in paroxysmal terms.

An analysis of events in the early 90s brings to mind the theoretical scheme formulated by economists to explain the slump which hit Europe at the start of the 80s. As the United States did one decade before, after unification Germany embarked on a course of expansive fiscal–tight money monetary policy. This helped to curb German domestic inflation and strengthened the D-mark, whereas it 'exported' inflationary and above all recessionary impulses to all other European countries who were obligated to retaliate with equally restrictive monetary policies. The persistently high unemployment rates in Europe (edging on 20% in Spain and Ireland, over 10% in Italy, UK and France, and just under 8% in Germany) may be partly explained by these facts as well as by technological change and competition from newly industrialized countries with low labour costs.

Jozzo, 1993

Despite this gloomy picture, Pierre-André Buigues,[3] in a masterly collaborative study, does nonetheless see important sectoral comparative advantages among EC Member States. We shall return to this optimistic study at the end of this chapter.

AFTER THE TREATY ON EUROPEAN UNION

As already mentioned, in this Treaty detailed plans were laid down only for the EMU. The part of these plans which has created the most furore (apart from the idiotic timetable – to which I shall turn in a moment) are the incredibly stiff criteria for Member States wishing to enter the final stage of the EMU. These are as follows:

(i)   government deficit spending (the national budget) shall not exceed
      3 per cent of gross domestic product (GDP) at market prices,

(ii) government debt shall not exceed 60 per cent of GDP at market
      prices,

(iii) inflation for a country over one year before examination shall not
      exceed by more than 1.5 per cent 'that of at most the three best
      performing Member States in terms of price stability',

(iv) a country must be a member of the ERM and must not have
      experienced serious upheavals in the two preceding years, and,

(v)   in the preceding year, a Member State shall have had an average
      nominal long-term interest rate that does not exceed by more than
      2 per cent 'that of, at most, the three best performing Member States
      in terms of price stability'.

At the time of writing, only Luxemburg fulfils all five criteria! Maybe
Luxemburg holds the key to the future – we shall see. Luxemburg is
closely followed by Denmark and France, both of whose currencies are
under semi-constant pressure.

      Then, there is the question of the timetable. As I wrote to the
Financial Times in July 1992, such a schedule is a lot of dangerous
nonsense. But, I also believe that there has been a conspiracy of
silence and legalistic ignorance about this matter. Hence, if we refer to
article 109 J, sections 3 to 5, of the Treaty, we read the following:

3. *Taking due account of the reports referred to in paragraph 1 and the*
opinion of the European Parliament referred to in paragraph 2, the
Council, meeting in the composition of Heads of State or of Government,
shall, acting by a qualified majority, not later than 31 December 1996:

decide, on the basis of the recommendations of the Council referred to in paragraph 2, whether a majority of the Member States fulfil the necessary conditions for the adoption of a single currency;

decide whether it is appropriate for the Community to enter the third stage, and if so,

set the date for the beginning of the third stage.

4. If by the end 1997 the date for the beginning of the third stage has not been set, the third stage shall start on 1 January 1999. Before 1 July 1998, the Council, meeting in the composition of Heads of State or of Government, after a repetition of the procedure provided for in paragraphs 1 and 2, with the exception of the second indent of paragraph 2, taking into account the reports referred to in paragraph 1 and the opinion of the European Parliament, shall, acting by a qualified majority and on the basis of the recommendations of the Council referred to in paragraph 2, confirm which Member States fulfill the necessary conditions for the adoption of a single currency.

Treaty on European Union, 1992

Thus, it is only if the date for the beginning of the final phase has not been agreed upon by the end of 1997 that it shall start on 1 January 1999. But, the ministers could decide on 1 July 2015, for example.

Then there is the question of the impending creation of the European Monetary Institute which will, apparently, lead to the setting-up of a European Central Bank (ECB). Where will the site of this ECB be? Well, it could be Bonn. . . and why not Strasburg or Lyons or Edinburgh? In the meantime, where they are not independent 'à la Bundesbank', the central banks of the EC Member States have to become independent. At the time of writing, most Member States have already accomplished this or are in the process of doing so. However, the question of accountability of central banks has never been examined. If we take the example of the Bundesbank, it is not accountable to Parliament. Is this a model which the future European Union (EU) should emulate?

FUTURE ECONOMIC AND MONETARY UNION

Inevitably, the moves of the Community and other European countries towards the establishing a full EMU should and will be a process of 'Europe à la carte' because of differences in national preferences and structure and the results of past and present economic and monetary policies. Furthermore, if these countries wish to achieve a full EMU then a situation similar to that existing in Luxemburg will have to develop. What do I mean by this? First, Luxemburg is very open and is almost completely integrated economically with the rest of the EC. Thus, that country is already part of a United Community. Whilst I do not think it will be necessary for the rest of the EC Member States to trade 100 per cent of their GDP with each other, I believe we should be approaching a level of 70 per cent before we can talk of real integration.

Second, if the Community continues to insist on Member States fulfilling the five severe criteria for membership of a full EMU, then the others will have to emulate Luxemburg. Otherwise, the Community will have to modify these rules. Whatever happens, some countries, as has always been the case, will move more swiftly towards a full EMU than others. For example, were it not for the heavy public debts of Belgium and the Netherlands, then the Benelux countries could form an EMU with Germany fairly soon.

Then, there is the question of a European currency – or the present European Currency Unit (ECU).[4] Despite the unexpected success of the commercial ECU, this currency unit is not widely used – especially not in trade. Consequently, I feel that, if and when we do have a common European currency, it will, at least for number of years, be a parallel currency alongside the present national currencies of the EC Member States. In the long run, however, as these countries become more integrated there will be more pressure and desire for the use of a common currency which, internationally, would reflect the Community's tremendous lead in international trade.

And, job creation, what should we do? Now everyone is talking about this problem – whether it be at the Tokyo Summit in June, or in the OECD Annual Report on Employment in July, this year. This concern has gone hand-in-hand with the already mentioned public deficits and the high costs of social security and employment taxes in some countries. One common element which applies to many but not all European countries is the availability of, and access to, training of quality. Personally, I would favour the adoption of the German example whereby an unemployed person receives benefits at the level of the last salary, provided he or she trains for a new job. Certainly, the automatic provision of welfare benefits which condemns individuals (especially young persons) to a state of permanent unemployment is both morally and economically wrong.

POSSIBLE OPTIMISM FOR THE FUTURE

Having spent far, far too many years in Amsterdam, I must be both an incurable optimist and a masochist! However, despite my basic optimistic nature, I do detect some optimistic signs for the future. Why should I be optimistic? I believe that the present concern about unemployment and public deficits will force governments to adopt policies concerning unemployment benefits like the German model.

Then, there are technological and trade possibilities which most experts have overlooked. The opening-up of the internal telecommunications markets of the EC Member States in 1998 will cause an explosion of investment. Certainly that is the view of the Chairman of the great American corporation AT&T. [5] Similarly, all East European countries and those of the former Soviet Union must be re-equipped with modern communications systems and a new transport infrastructure. Here much of the equipment must come from the West. Finally, trade barriers are falling, and, given the right economic climate, the different EC sectors could use much more of their comparative advantage as described by Pierre-André Buigues. But, we must adopt a system of 'product differentiation', so frequently mentioned by Alexis Jacquemin, whereby we manufacture those products (and, of course, purvey those services) more in keeping with our levels of education and technology – that is the real reason why I am critical of the Community's CAP.

As I shall stress in the conclusions of this book, the EC and EFTA

Member States are for the most part highly developed technological societies with well-educated and frequently well-trained citizens. They possess sophisticated infrastructures and a wonderful cultural life. Consequently, the problem we face is that of releasing these talents and energies and using them in the optimum manner. This is one of the reasons for the present interest in the efficacy or otherwise of our social security systems. It is also the main reason for my criticism of the wastefulness of the EC's CAP.

Then, there is the question as to whether the present moves towards creating an EMU will lead to the optimum use of our talents and resources. The recent experience with the EMS plus the high levels of unemployment in EC countries (due also to the world recession and extravagant social security systems), seem to suggest that we are either on the wrong track or that we are trying to implement the EMU in the wrong way or that some EC and EFTA Member States may be stronger candidates for an EMU than others.

Personally, I think there is a mixture of reasons for our present problems and that we are clearly not using our resources in an optimum manner. Also, as I have just explained, some countries are indeed more likely candidates for an EMU than others. Thus, in the foreseeable future, it is desirable and inevitable that we shall create an EMU on an à la carte basis.

FOOTNOTE

Following tremendous pressure in the exchange markets on the French Franc and the Danish and Spanish currencies, the EMS and ERM were restructured on Sunday 1 August 1993. The new system, which came into being the following day, comprised a band of fluctuation of 15 per cent on either side of the central parity. Exclusively for Germany and the Netherlands, the old margin of fluctuation of 2.25 per cent remained in force.

NOTES

1. Especially: P. Coffey, 1987, *The European Monetary System– Past, Present and Future*, Dordrecht, Netherlands: Kluwer Academic Publishers.
2. Alfonso Jozzo, 1993, ECU Newsletter, Turin, Italy, March.
3. P. Buigues, F. Ilzkovitz and J-F LeBrun, 1991, *L'Impact Sectoriel du Marché Intérieur Sur L'Industriel*, Paris: Economia.
4. As of 23 November 1992, the composition of the ECU is as follows:

Deutsche Mark	31.69%
French Franc	20.16%
Pound Sterling	10.90%
Dutch Guilder	9.90%
Italian Lira	8.98%
*Belgian Franc	8.44%
Spanish Peseta	4.80%
Danish Crown	2.63%
Irish Pound	1.16%
Portuguese Escudo	.76%
Greek Drachma	.57%

   * Includes the Luxemburg Franc

5. See interview with Bob Allen, Chairman of AT&T, *Financial Times*, 19 July 1993.

10. A Common Foreign Policy?

The aim of having a common foreign policy for the European Community – as laid down in the Treaty on European Union – together with the Community's chaotic and disagreeable lack of policy for Bosnia, make this a particularly difficult chapter to write. And yet, amid my deep dismay and shame at the Community's behaviour *vis-à-vis* Bosnia, I do discern two areas where we do, and have for some time, a common foreign policy. These two areas are trade and defence of the geographical integrity of the EC Member States.

THE TRADE DIMENSION

Writing in 1992,[1] I analysed the Community's trading policies in the following terms. The twelve Community Member States are mainly highly developed countries and they are either open or very open economies (see Table 9.1). They form the most highly integrated regional grouping in the world – conducting some 60 per cent of their trade with each other. Unlike the United States, and, with the recent exceptions of Britain and the Netherlands – with their discoveries of North Sea oil and natural gas (though, it is true that the Netherlands has enjoyed the bonanza of the important Groningen reserves of natural gas for the past 30 years – responsible, in part, for the financing of the lavish Dutch social welfare programme) – the EC Member States do not possess their own resources of energy and raw materials. In this sense, they are more similar to Japan than to the United States.

Unlike both Japan and the United States, at the end of World War II, four countries of the European Community were major colonial powers. In fact, Portugal remained just such a power until 1975! This fact, as we shall see later in this chapter, was to have a major influence on the Community's external economic policies and relations that have lasted until this present day.

Then, of course, there is the EC's Common Agricultural Policy (CAP). To the author, it is this policy that has influenced, negatively, our external economic relations with all countries – except with Thailand, and, currently and temporarily (hopefully), the countries of the former Soviet Union. Nowhere is the influence of the CAP more upsetting, and potentially more dangerous, than in our relations with the United States.

But, in all this, is there any particular logic in the Community's external economic relations? Speaking before representatives of the Commission of the European Comunities and of the ASEAN group of countries, in Brussels, in the Autumn of 1987, I reiterated the seven main principles influencing the Community's external economic relations and about which I had written some years earlier. These principles, which I still believe to be valid, are the following:

1. The EEC (with the recent exceptions of the Netherlands and the United Kingdom) is not self-sufficient in supplies of energy and raw materials. Therefore, these commodities have been allowed to enter the Community either free of duty or with very low tariffs.
2. At the end of the transitional period, the Common External Tariff (CET) would consist of the average of the existing (1957) tariffs of the Member States. Subsequent participation by the EC in a series of international negotiations have resulted in a rather low average CET.
3. It was agreed that special arrangements would be made for existing overseas territories, dependencies and the like for which Member States exercise responsibility. This policy has evolved over time from the special arrangements made for such countries to the two Yaoundé Agreements and further on the present and Fourth Lomé Agreement.
4. At the outset, the Community decided to embark upon the construction of a Common Agricultural Policy (CAP) and until the Common Agricultural Market (CAM) actually came into being the EEC was unwilling to discuss the question of agricultural matters in

international trade negotiations. Since the full achievement of the CAM, its existence has tended to negatively influence the Community's trade relations with most parts of the world especially with Eastern Europe, Australasia, Latin America and the United States.

5. The Community expressed its willingness to enter into international trade negotiations with non-Community countries. Subsequently, the EC has been (together with the USA and more recently, Japan) the principal protagonist in point 2, and, following the Tokyo Round Negotiations, the average CET is now rather low.

6. Partly, as a consequence of the low CET and partly due to the increased competitive ability of a growing number of Third World countries (particularly in the fields of clothing and textiles) the EC has, since the 1970s increasingly resorted to non-tariff barriers of a 'voluntarist' nature which are sometimes described as Orderly Marketing Arrangements (OMAs) or Voluntary Export Restrictions (VERs). Currently, efforts are being made to 'persuade' Japan to restrict exports of cars and electronic products to EC Member States.

7. Since the mid-1970s, the Community has started to move in the direction of attempting to secure its supplies of energy and raw materials. This more recent policy is an obvious reaction to the lack of self-sufficiency in these fields – which was mentioned in point 1.

Some of these points deserve further examination. Points 1 and 7 clearly influence the Community's attitude to a number of less-developed countries since they tend to be the EC's main sources of energy and raw materials. Thus, apart from the special historical links between the the Community and the African, Caribbean and Pacific (ACP) countries (to which we shall turn in a few moments), efforts have been made to make special arrangements with specific countries. One such example of this trend had been the Community's involvement with the important Carajás Iron Ore Project in Brazil. As a result of these links, Third World countries which supply the EC with energy and raw materials are vulnerable to the Community's fortunes. Some of these countries are also particularly interested in the possibility of enjoying the privileges conferred upon the 'chosen' Third World countries referred to under point 3.

At the meeting of the Council of Ministers held in Venice, in 1956, France had threatened not to join the nascent EEC if special arrangements were not made for her African territories. The reaction to this threat and the ensuing policies are with us to this present day. First, special arrangements were made for the African Associate States and Madagascar (AASM). Then, as these countries gained their independence, new arrangements were made (called the Yaoundé arrangements) which took the form of reciprocal preferential trading agreements – together with the transfer of financial aid (the ARUSHA arrangements were also made for three anglophone African states). Subsequently, when Britain joined the EEC, these arrangements were transformed into the Lomé Accords and extended to many former British colonies (more recently, also to the former Portuguese territories). However, these Lomé Accords – which are the object of criticism and envy by many Latin American countries – are different from their predecessors in that they are *non*-reciprocal and embody two very important arrangements, the STABEX (for traditional tropical products) and SYSMIN (for metals) arrangements. These aim, through the transfer of funds to the ACP states to compensate for falls in the prices of their listed exports under the STABEX and SYSMIN schemes, to maintain their export earnings. Furthermore, the lists of products under both these schemes are *non-definitive*.

But, the points which are of immediate consequence to us in this book are numbers 2, 4, 5, and, to some degree, point 6. As mentioned earlier, point 4, concerning the Community's CAP, is the point of greatest contention between the EC and the United States. Similarly, point 6 is brought into part of this chapter – but more extensively when examining the EC's policies for the Single European Market (SEM). How, then, does the Community translate these policies into action, and, can it be said to have clear preferences for specific individual countries or groups of states? Trade relations between the EC and third party countries are normally developed in one or a mixture of four ways:

(i) Through specific agreements between the EC and individual states or groups of countries. Here, an almost endless list of agreements is possible. These may take the form of association agreements which may or may not lead to eventual full membership of the Community. Such agreements may have a financial aid package attached to the them. Examples of the agreements extend from those made with Greece and Turkey, which in the former case, led to that country's full membership of the EC – to those recently made with several East European countries. There are preferential and non-preferential trade agreements. Such arrangements are normally reciprocal in nature – though the Lomé Accords are not. In the case of highly developed countries – for example, the European Free Trade Association (EFTA) – the normal arrangement offered would be a reciprocal free trade agreement. Then, for Third World countries, not associated with the coveted Lomé Accords, the most flexible arrangement would be a co-operative arrangement – which may or may not be linked with a financial and technical aid package. Such arrangements tend to be favoured for links between the Community and Latin American countries.

(ii) Through multilateral trade negotiations (MTNs). As already mentioned, together with the United States, the EC is the main protagonist in these negotiations.

(iii) Through the Generalized System of Preferences (GSPs). This arrangement, which is intended for Third World countries, takes the form of non-reciprocal tariff-free quotas for the exports of these countries to the more developed ones. Here, the Community is the most important developed participant and has recently extended the arrangement for a further decade.

(iv) Through the Multi-Fibre Agreement (MFA). This agreement was originally intended as a means of increasing, on a regular basis, textile exports of Third World countries to the more developed ones. Unfortunately, it has been transformed into a means of controlling exports of textiles from Third World countries. However, it is now intended to bring textiles back into the GATT fold – where they correctly belong.

So, which countries or groups of states are the Community's favourites and how are the associate privileges translated in to concrete results? Well, if we exclude the EC Member States themselves, I would choose the following list – in descending order of importance:

(i)   the EFTA countries,
(ii)   the ACP States,
(iii)   the Mediterranean countries – notably the Mahgreb States,
(iv)   the United States,
(v)   the others – including non-ACP Third World countries – and
        Japan.

What is most surprising is that, despite the privileges conferred on the ACP States (some 76 countries), they do not, as a bloc, constitute the most important trading partner of the EC. Rather, the United States is the Community's number one trading partner. Similarly, the EC is the most important trading partner of the United States.

Amid all these internal and external economic and trading policies, one thing is certain. The Community, apart from being the world's largest trading bloc, is also the main protagonist in the MTNs in the framework of the GATT. At the present time, the confrontation in the Uruguay Round is between the United States and the EC. To reach any agreement in the MTNs, agreement between the two trade superpowers is absolutely indispensable. And until the very recent murmur of discord raised by France regarding the compromise reached at Blair House by the two sides late last year, the Community has, since the Kennedy Round, spoken with one voice and has consequently been able to gain major trade concessions. Apart from the present French dissent, but since the achievement of many of the aims associated with the Single European Market, the Community could find its international negotiating position considerably strengthened.

TERRITORIAL INTEGRITY

For those EC Member States which are members of NATO and WEU, their territorial integrity in Europe is assured . . . but what about their overseas territories?

Although no policy had been enunciated for such areas, when, in 1982, Argentina invaded the Falkland Islands, the Community, with the understandable exceptions of Italy, Spain and Ireland, regarded the Argentine invasion as an attack on its territory. Thus, economic and trade relations with that country were broken. The effectiveness of this policy was borne out by the energy used by Argentina to have relations with EC Member States restored at the end of hostilities. We can therefore assume that the Community will not, in future, allow the violation of the overseas territories of any of its Member States.

BOSNIA

In future years, we shall pay dearly for the blindness and scandalous selfishness of the EC Member States – but especially the short-sightedness of Britain and France – in the Bosnian crisis. I shall not waste time talking about the Community's misguided desire to maintain the integrity of the former Yugoslavia, but, once one recognizes the territorial integrity of a European country, one has a moral and practical obligation to defend it. To do anything less is to lose all one's credibility. Unfortunately, John Major and François Mitterand have learned nothing from history. In Bosnia, we have a repetition of both the Spanish Civil War and the Nazi annexation of the Sudetenland in Czechoslovakia. In the case of Spain, France and Britain forbade the supply of arms to the Republican Government whereas the Nazis and Italian Fascists were free to help Franco. In the case of Czechoslovakia, the Franco-British betrayal of Czechoslovakia simply postponed the real military confrontation with the Nazis for a year.

In our shameful and unbelievably short-sighted policies we have done three things:

1. We have shown that no European country outside the EC and NATO can count on our military help if attacked.
2. The Community has shown that aggression pays off very well indeed.
3. Although the Bosnian Muslims were never fanatical in a religious sense (many were, in fact, not practising Muslims at all), we have, in our betrayal of them, created future terrorists who will cause us great harm. Furthermore, we have seriously damaged our relations with Muslim countries.

THE FUTURE

Outside the area of foreign trade, notably in the field of the MTNs, and the question of the territorial integrity of EC Member States, I do not see the evolution of a common foreign policy by the Community in the forseeable future. Instead, I see the development, as in the monetary field, of à la carte policies whereby those Member States which feel that they have common international interests will tend to act together. One example here is the close historical relations which already existed, and which are currently being intensified, between Portugal and Spain and Latin American countries. Here, also, the Community does have bilateral trade and co-operation agreements with individual Latin American countries – as well as with regional groupings in that part of the world.

I do, however, note a major positive development in the case of the Community's redoubtable foreign policy weapon – trade. Recently, in the co-operation agreements which have been made between the EC and countries in Central America – as well as with countries in Eastern Europe and elsewhere – the Community has laid down specific conditions relating to moves towards parliamentary democracy as well as respect for human rights. My impression is that this will henceforth be the norm for future EC co-operation agreements and will strongly influence the preparations for the next and fifth Lomé Accord. These developments had already been taking place before the signing of the Treaty on European Union. They imply that the Community was already unanimously adopting a much more energetic and qualitative common foreign trade policy.

To me, this is a realistic and particularly positive foreign policy development which is effective because it is based on unanimity. Thus there exists a common basis for those Member States which wish to pursue other types of foreign policy and security aims on an à la carte basis.

In Europe itself, the Community would, nevertheless, do well to learn a necessary lesson from the Bosnian tragedy. Henceforth, when it recognizes a European country, it should clearly state its intention of defending the frontiers of that state.

NOTES

1. Peter Coffey, 1993, *The EC and the United States*, Dordrecht: Kluwer Academic Publishers.

11. The Military Dimension

Despite major reductions in arms by the superpowers, but because of the breakup of the former Soviet Union and other countries in Eastern and Central Europe, at no time since 1945 has it been necessary for Western European countries to have a coherent military policy backed up by forces of high quality – *at their immediate disposal*. Failure to put into effect such a policy immediately will make us pay dearly in the years to come. But, if we are to have a common and coherent military policy, what should be its basic tenets?

Probably the most cogent list has been laid down by René Van Beveren.[1] He suggests that:

> States have a common defence policy when an agreement exists on the aims of the engagement of armed forces. Various measures in preparation for that engagement can be taken, ranging from studies by military staffs to the drawing up of detailed operational plans to meet different contingencies but the engagement itself will be executed through ad hoc arrangements.
>
> For defence to be considered 'common', the states concerned must at least have a centralised military structure which is ready to assume command of the armed forces involved in each engagement. This common defence can extend to the procurement of defence equipment and even the permanent integration of units from different nations in one command.
>
> Van Beveren, 1993

THE PRESENT SITUATION

To me, the key element in this definition is the reference to a 'centralised military structure'. At the present time only NATO fulfils this important criterion (although neither France nor Spain are under the central command). The defect in this centralized command is that the top command positions are held by Americans – we shall return to this point later in this chapter. However, as I have stated since 1989, NATO is the sole stable military organ in the whole of Europe. Consequently, even if its role will be changed, it should, both qualitatively and quantitatively, remain strong. But, what is its most urgent and immediate task? Clearly, at the present time, the most important element in NATO's tactical arsenal is, and will increasingly be, the Rapid Deployment Force (RDF). According to Bernard Adam,[2] various estimates by experts suggest that, in order to meet all possible contingencies, we need a force of between 150,000 and 350,000 men. At the present time, we have about 70,000 men at our disposal of whom 60 per cent are provided by the United Kingdom.

The Western European Union (WEU) and the Franco-German Defence Corps have an important potential role in the creation of a future, more specifically European, RDF. The Treaty on European Union does envisage a major role here for the WEU but here there are two different views regarding the precise position of this organization *vis-à-vis* NATO. Thus, whilst Britain and Italy want it to be an arm of NATO, France and Germany have tended to prefer a more independent European role for the WEU – though, more recently, their attitude seems to be changing.

Then, there is the question of the Franco–German Defence Corps.[3] Personally, and perhaps wrongly, I believe this body to be more symbolic than real. This corps, which will not be operational until 1 October 1995, will comprise 35,000 men. France and Germany have invited other European countries to join this force, and, in June 1993, Belgium and Spain expressed their intention of so doing. A positive development is the agreement, signed by France and Germany, which will operate within the framework of the Alliance. However, the most disquieting feature about the Euro–Corps, apart from its size, its date of operation and the quarrels about its operating languages, is the fact that the participating countries use different armaments systems. Furthermore, there are no plans, as yet, to harmonize these systems.

A PAN-EUROPEAN FRAMEWORK

Many observers had, rightly or wrongly, hoped that the Conference on Security and Co-operation in Europe (CSCE) would create a Pan-European framework for peace and military co-operation. Unfortunately, this is a large and unwieldy body, and, when in May 1992, Russia vetoed a proposal to temporarily exclude Yugoslavia from the Conference, its inflexibility was underlined.

More recently, France has made a proposal for a draft Pact on Security and Stability in Europe which was presented to the European Council in Copenhagen on 21 and 22 June. This Pact, which 35 European countries (plus five associates) would be eligible to join, aims at preventing another Bosnian crisis in Europe. To what degree might such a Pact be capable of preventing the development of similar crises in future? On a first reading of the proposals,[4] I find that of the three aims (A, B and C) the second one on Minority Rights is of great urgency. However, on looking more closely at the proposals, I find a lack of clarity. Thus, the following statement on the Consolidation of Borders is woolly and possibly dangerous.

A. Consolidation of borders

The preparatory conference should not limit its action to solemnly reaffirming the inviolability of borders in Europe. It must lead to the conclusion of friendship agreements founded on respect for the rights of minorities, since the violation of these rights risks causing international complications.

Without taking sides a priori, the possibility cannot be ruled out that these agreements may lead to minor rectifications of borders, the intangibility of which would then be established by the conference. The states participating in the conference would thus collectively serve as guarantors of these bilateral agreements.

European Documents, 1993

This section, I fear, runs the risk of repeating the mistakes of the Helsinki Declaration – with the results we all know.

The aims regarding minorities, as set down below, are indeed noble. However, I fear that they are only good intentions because I do not see the provision of any really effective means of putting them into effect.

B. Minorities

With respect to principles, existing texts have gradually evolved from a purely individual conception of the rights of persons belonging to minorities towards a conception taking account of their collective aspect and the very close tie linking them to security problems.

At the present time, nationals of Council of Europe member countries have the *right of individual appeal* in regard to the European Convention on Human Rights. The 'Court of Conciliation and Arbitration', ratification of which by the interested countries must be hastened, can deal with *disputes between states*. Finally, the High Commissioner for National Minorities existing within the CSCE can examine the *collective rights of a minority*.

Pursuing this evolution, the conference preparing the Pact would examine a report requested by the Twelve of the High Commissioner for National Minorities and would set as an objective to be attained within a given period (eight months):

leading the Eastern and Central European countries to set out among themselves agreements of a nature to provide practical solutions on a case-by-case basis to their minority problems. This examination would take place by regional sub-units, the states directly concerned associating other members of the conference whose presence would be accepted as moderators.

setting out preventive procedures capable of keeping violations of rights of minorities from leading to security problems. The role of powers of the *High Commissioner for National Minorities* should be reappraised. Should the High Commissioner play a role of adviser for minorities so as to make better known *all the institutional mechanisms capable of ensuring their satisfactory presentation* (means of election, presence in the administrative hierarchy, arrangements for coexistence between regions, etc.)? How can preventative action be more effective? Should the Commissioner also have a right of appeal and before what body? (Would the Summit of Heads of State of the Twelve agree to hear the Commissioner once a year?)

European Documents, 1993

And how are these aims to be achieved? As already mentioned, I do not really see any concrete measures in these proposals. When examining the section on Incentives and Flanking Measures, the only possible, potentially long-term, dynamic step which proposed is future co-operation between Central and Eastern European countries, the 12 EC Member States, NATO and WEU (I shall return to this possibility at the end of this chapter). But, as the text below indicates, the authors do not view the imposition of sanctions with any degree of enthusiasm. Personally, I think that this is a defeatist view since sanctions imposed totally and with energy by the Community can succeed.

C. Incentives and flanking measures

The preparatory conference should examine the best way to lead European countries to respect the principles to which they adhere and propose flanking measures that could be taken to encourage peace and stability in Europe.

The incentives and flanking measures depending essentially on the will of the Twelve are:

political: to respond to the expectations of Central European countries and certain East European countries, the Community would contemplate *eventual new memberships, on the express condition that, within the framework of the conference,* the problems likely to threaten European stability are resolved. This condition, of course, would be necessary but not sufficient. The Community would have to determine whether these countries are in a position to become members.

economic: can the Community decide to provide specific assistance to countries taking particular care to solve their problems relating to minorities (for accompanying projects in specific regions), immigration or refugees (setting up resettlement programmes)? In the opposite case, can it also decide to *cut off all cooperation ties with a country flagrantly violating the rights of minorities or calling existing borders into question?* The Yugoslav experience shows that such incentives have their limits when they are not implemented in timely fashion.

The preparatory conference should examine the *flanking measures* that could be taken to encourage this stability in a preventive way.

More precisely, it could:

study the possibility for the WEU to admit as associate members the countries adhering to a European agreement whose membership in the European Union is an eventual possibility and to develop military cooperation with them, notably in the area of peacekeeping. Could units available rapidly for this type of operation be designated in advance?

foster military cooperation among Central and Eastern European countries, the Twelve, NATO and the WEU.

propose practical measures to strengthen the CSCE institutions.

European Documents, 1993

The first reaction of the European Council was to invite the Council (General Affairs) to examine the proposals and to prepare and present a report to the Council meeting at the end of the year with a view to calling a preparatory conference to examine these findings – another conference!

At a more immediate and practical level, outside a building up of NATO's RDF, existing co-operation between some EC Member States is being and will continue to be deepened. Here, the most notable example is that of France and Britain who have been co-operating in the area of joint production and procurement of conventional weapons and who are now co-operating in the field of nuclear weapons. It is to the question of these weapons to which we shall now turn.

THE NUCLEAR NIGHTMARE

It is no exaggeration to call the present nuclear situation in Europe a nightmare – yet it is a totally different one from the danger of a possible nuclear conflict between the superpowers, but fought on European soil, which some of us feared in the 1960s and 1970s. Rather, our present nightmare concerns the unwillingness of the Ukraine to get rid of the 176 strategic missiles on its soil, since that country regards these armaments as constituting 'national property'. As if this were not enough, the Ukraine is blocking the implementation of the second Strategic Arms Reductions Treaty (START II, signed in 1992) by which the long-range nuclear arsenals of Russia and the US would be reduced by about two-thirds to about 3,500 each, by the beginning of the twenty-first century. The problem here is that the Ukraine has not ratified the previous START I Treaty of 1991 on which the present START II is constructed. Furthermore, the Ukraine is delaying signing the Non-Proliferation Treaty (NPT) of 1968. But another former member of the Soviet Union, Kazakhstan, though it has ratified START I, has not signed the NPT.

This is a very worrying situation since, whilst the present leaders of these two countries seem to be reasonable men, we are not sure what their future leaders will be like. To me, the solution would be for the West to offer major financial help to both countries to de-activate and destroy these missiles (we are told that the Ukraine is trying to break the codes which are used to activate these missiles).

But, what of the nuclear military power of Western Europe? Whilst we have relied heavily on the US nuclear umbrella since the end of World War II, we cannot now take this protection for granted in view of the present *détente* between Russia and the US. This leaves us with the British and French nuclear deterrents. As mentioned earlier, both countries are collaborating in the nuclear field. Apart from this co-operation, it would, in the first instance, be a policy measure of the greatest importance if France and Britain would offer to defend any EC Member State, if they should request such help, when facing an external attack. Over time, this offer could be extended to other European countries.

FUTURE POLICIES – MY PROPOSALS

According to the most recent report of the Oslo-based International Peace Research Institute,[5] the number of global armed conflicts increased substantially in 1992 – and many of these took place in Europe. Furthermore, the report suggests that present (1992) minor conflicts in such countries as Georgia and Moldavia are likely, in future, to become much more protracted. Consequently, to me, we are living in a transitional period of great danger when we need more weapons and/or troops of a specific type and quality in selected areas. Since, then, peace is no longer (or was it ever?) a natural state of affairs, I would make the following policy proposals:

1. The RDF of NATO should be immediately substantially increased in size.

2. The WEU should be an arm of NATO but with the possibility of its members being able to engage in independent action inside Europe.

3. The future Franco-German Euro-Corps should be integrated into the WEU and should be placed under centralized command.

4. As already proposed, Western European countries should immediately offer substantial financial help to the Ukraine and Kazakhstan to help them get rid of their nuclear missiles.

5. As a medium-term objective, and where feasible, NATO should offer military protection to the countries of Central and Eastern Europe.

6. As a long-term objective, where feasible, NATO should aim at bringing in these countries as members of the Alliance. [6]

7. Since, correctly, the US expects Europe to assume a greater responsibility for its defence, it would be reasonable for the top commander in NATO to be a European.

8. As an extension of point 5, long-term moves should be activated whereby East European countries (with the consent of Russia) would become members of NATO. As a more ambitious move, Russia's eventual membership of NATO should be envisaged.

Regarding point 8, in August 1992, *Le Monde* reported that Russia had apparently indicated that it had no objection to Poland's membership of NATO. If this report is true, this is indeed a most momentous development.

NOTES

1. René Van Beveren, 1993, *Military Cooperation: What Structure for the Future?*, Chaillot Papers No. 6, January, Paris: WEU.
2. Bernard Adam 1993, in *Memento Défense – Désarmament 1993*, Brussels: GRIP.
3. It should be noted that a small very symbolic Franco-German Force does already exist and is stationed in Strasburg.
4. *Europe Documents*, No. 1846, 26 June 1993, Brussels: Agence Europe.
5. P. Wallensteen and K. Axell, 1993, *Armed Conflict at the End of the Cold War, 1989-92*, Uppsala University, Sweden: Department of Peace and Conflict Research.
6. This aim is not so far fetched as it may seem at first sight since NATO established a Council for co-operation with these countries in 1990.

12. The Social Policy Issue

Having lain dormant for over a decade, social policy has become an urgently topical issue. Although it is an issue which affects citizens in both Eastern and Western Europe, I am, because of my inadequate knowledge about this area in Eastern Europe, restricting my examination to Western Europe. Basically, there are three main reasons for the current renewal of interest by governments and academics in social policy. These reasons are:

(i) The present unacceptably high levels of unemployment in nearly all West European countries. Although this phenomenon also affects older workers, it is of particular concern to younger citizens.

(ii) The unacceptably increasing costs of social security, and, in particular, the escalating costs of healthcare throughout the Western world – with the partial exception of the United Kingdom.

(iii)Then, there was and is the increasing concern of Jacques Delors that the EC should not simply be a community of producers but also one where the fundamental basic rights of workers are both carefully enunciated and confirmed at Community level. The concern of M. Delors resulted in the enunciation of the EC's Social Charter at the end of 1989 which was accepted by all EC Member States except Britain (the Charter is reproduced at the end of this book). Subsequently, the tenets of the Charter were embodied in the Treaty on European Union.

Europe is then facing a fundamental tension between the rights of workers, on the one hand, and the costs of maintaining and/or supporting these rights on the other hand. It is therefore reasonable and logical to first ascertain these rights. Fundamental human rights, which include the right to education and work, are clearly laid down in the European Convention on Human Rights, to which, in October 1993, 32 European countries became signatories. It is, however, to the EC's Social Charter to which I wish to turn my first examination.

Until the acceptance of the Social Charter, apart from only partially successful moves to establish equal rights between men and women (as laid down in article 119 of the Rome Treaty and in the constitutions of some EC Member States), social rights were those laid down for nationals of EC Member States migrating between these countries for purposes of work. Here, apart from the outlawing of discrimination between nationals of different EC Member States (except in the civil service – which is now opening up), the basic rights consisted of giving the same social security rights to the migrant (from another EC Member State) as those enjoyed by the citizens of the receiving country. Thus, the basic rights (apart from the question of equal rights) were laid down for migrant workers. With the acceptance of the Social Charter (with the exception of Britain) basic rights are laid down for all workers in the EC – whether they are migrants or not. This is then a major transformation.

The Charter itself is a noble document. In general, it lays down the basic rights which all workers should enjoy in any civilized society. There are, however, two areas which might lead to confusion and/or tensions. These are the reference to an 'equitable wage' and the freedom of association. Both these points were the reason for Britain's refusal to accept the Charter. The idea of an 'equitable wage' is not absolutely clear. In the Charter, the explanation given is, 'a wage sufficient to enable them to have a decent standard of living'. But, what precisely is the standard? Rightly or wrongly, Mrs. Thatcher saw this as being the eventual imposition of a guaranteed minimum European wage on EC Member States – with all the accompanying negative economic implications for poorer countries and regions in the Community. More recently, the EC Commission has tried (unsuccessfully, I would maintain) to make more clear the meaning of an 'equitable wage'. In its proposal to the Council of Ministers[1] (reproduced in full at the end of this book), the Commission repeats the criterion whereby a wage is 'fair and sufficient to enable them (the workers) to have a decent standard of living'. Again, this is not clearly explained: what is meant by a 'decent standard of living'? There are calls for investment in education and training and for equality of treatment (between men and women) and non-discrimination in general. Basically speaking, we are still left in the dark as to the precise meaning of an 'equitable wage'.

In contrast, the meaning and implementation of worker representation is both clear and vigorous. The impetus for including this in the Social Charter came from Germany where worker consultation and participation in the workplace have long been standard practice. This contrasts very much with Britain where it is certainly not desired by employers and not supported by many workers.

Thus, with varying degrees of clarity, workers' rights are now laid down inside the EC. At a more immediate level, however, the two most pressing current and future problems are the high levels of unemployment and the increasing costs of social security and healthcare. Unemployment is a costly and unacceptable waste of human talent. Inside the EC this crisis is compounded by the fact that it is also a regional and national problem. Although the Community has doubled the resources devoted to regional and social policies over the past five years and has agreed to do the same for the coming five years,[2] I still do not see any clear EC regional policy. We shall turn to this question later in the chapter.

What, then, should we and can we do about the present levels of unemployment? The clue to a possible solution to the present dilemma may be found (partially, at least) in Germany where, until the unification of the two Germanies, unemployment was very low (it is still low when compared with most EC countries). What are the possible reasons for this situation? Germany still has a substantial manufacturing base which tends to support the warnings of Alexis Jacquemin about 'dis-industrialization' in Europe. Apart from Germany's record of high productivity, of equal importance are the facts that the Germans tend to produce goods with a higher value added and of a quality that reflects the country's levels of education, but even more so, of training. Against all this must be set the lavish social security benefits and long holidays enjoyed by workers – which the heads of business enterprises and the German Government are currently trying to curtail. Can and should the German experience be taken as a model for the rest of Western Europe? Yes and no. I do not think we can transpose a set of traditions from one European country to another. An example of this difficulty is the case of Ireland which has a highly educated young workforce and sophisticated new industries – but a very high level of unemployment – which is compounded by the inevitable high birth rates in the Republic.

Nevertheless, there is general agreement throughout Western Europe that we need a highly educated, well-trained and flexible workforce, which, together with high and judicious levels of capital investment, will enable us to adopt a policy of 'product differentiation', as proposed by Alexis Jacquemin. But this will necessitate an active regional policy. This policy should be concerned with the enhancement of the infrastructure inside Western Europe and the promotion of small and medium-sized enterprises. As the European Parliament suggested in 1977, an active Community Regional Policy should favour the creation of 'development poles', as has long been the policy in France, whereby over periods of up to thirty years major regional capitals would be developed – economically and culturally – to counteract the pull of the capital cities. To some degree, with varying degrees of success, a similar policy has been adopted by the former West Germany – with its creation of *schwerpunkten* – and in Italy with the *progetto 80*.

Certainly a more co-ordinated and dynamic structural regional policy with specific aims would be preferable to the present situation, where, apart from the small 'non-compulsory' part of the European Regional Fund where the Commission can inaugurate its own projects, the Community simply co-finances local and national initiatives.

Naturally, the increased financing of educational, training and structural projects will mean that account must be taken of the increasing degree of spending on social security and healthcare. What, then, are the principles involved, what are the reasons for our present dilemma and what should we do in the future with social security?

Social security is essentially based on one or both of two principles: social welfare and/or social insurance. The basic ideas about social welfare were laid down in the Beveridge Report in Britain in World War II. According to these principles, no citizen should fall below a certain minimum of welfare and the State should be responsible for ensuring that this does not happen. It was this report and its inherent principles which largely influenced the building of Britain's National Health Service which gives health coverage for the whole population, and which, like the rest of social security, is heavily financed from the national budget. This mode of financing has also been adopted by Denmark and Ireland. Whatever the means of financing the system, throughout Western Europe it is accepted that there is a minimum degree of welfare below which no citizen should fall and that no one should be refused medical assistance for financial reasons. Consequently, social welfare no longer presents a major problem. In contrast, the concept of social insurance is quite different. Here, benefits are linked to contributions and length of service. In recent years, there has also been a tendency to link the benefits with inflation ('indexation'). Naturally, this has pushed up the costs of social security. The costs to which I have just referred have been further increased by rising unemployment, the ageing of the population, and, in some countries, the ever-increasing and insatiable demands of the population for medicines and pills of every conceivable size and colour. The last mentioned case has been underlined by the recent OECD study[3] which used the example of France where under the health system patients can visit their doctors as often as they please. Doctors are paid a fee for each consultation and produce an ever-increasing number of prescriptions. However, the same study does stress that most of the countries examined are trying to contain healthcare costs. In particular, on the side of cost containment and quality of services, it refers to the British example where part of hospital budgets are given to some large (competing) general practices – thus allowing them to shop around for hospital services for their patients. Similarly, the British practice of a set annual fee per patient for doctors and the bulk (contract) buying of medicines and pills tends to further reduce costs. This question of costs will become more acute over time because Europe's population – with the exception of Ireland and Turkey and the partial exception of Britain – is an ageing one.   Consequently, not only will we have populations expecting and needing more healthcare, over a longer period of time, but there will be fewer active people to support them. What is being done and what should we do about this problem?

As already examined, the problem of unemployment is the most pressing. If we reduce the numbers of the unemployed we shall reduce costs and increase revenue. Apart from the structural regional measures already proposed, we could do the following (in some countries it is already happening) in order to induce greater flexibility and mobility among workers as well as creating new employment opportunities:

1. In some countries, notably France, the social security contributions paid by employers are unacceptably high. A reduction in these taxes would encourage businesses to engage more workers.
2. Where possible, the British policy of cost containment of healthcare costs should be adopted throughout Western Europe.
3. In the field of healthcare, emphasis should be put on preventative medicine.
4. Current rules about the 'indexation' of social security benefits should be modified. Here, recent Italian changes in social legislation are most encouraging.
5. In many West European countries, tenure of employment is sacrosanct – even where a worker commits professional errors. A modification of these laws should make it possible to engage younger and more dynamic workers.
6. In countries where there is a heavily ageing population (e.g. Germany: according to OECD studies, there will be an age dependency ratio of 34 per cent by the year 2040), older workers should be discouraged from taking early retirement.
7. One of the ever-increasing costs of social security is state pensions. Here, I would propose a dual solution of making pensions more income-related, and, once again, encouraging older workers to stay on longer in full-time employment.

I do not believe for one moment that the proposals constitute a panacea for all our problems. Thus, for example, if we want more mobility for workers, we will need a more flexible housing policy which will encourage the provision of more rented accommodation. Equally, I am aware that there will be great resistance among workers and others to some of these proposals. Nevertheless, their adoption should encourage the private sector to provide the job possibilities (as is the case in the United States) which the public sector has been unable to do in recent years. Personally, I do not believe that the present social problem in Western Europe is one of guaranteeing basic rights – rather it is a combined problem of increasing job possibilities and cutting social security costs.

NOTES

1. Commission Opinion on an Equitable Wage, Official Journal, 93/C248/04, Com (93) 388 Final, 1 September 1993.
2. The amount of EC regional aid allocated for the period 1994-99 is 157 billion ECUs. As during the period 1989-93, the main beneficiaries will be Greece, Ireland, Portugal and Spain.
3. OECD, 1992, *The Reform of Health Care*, Paris.

13. The Rights of Citizens:
European Citizenship, Migration and Related Issues

The rights of citizens – which citizens? No question could possibly be more controversial at the present time – yet an acceptable answer to this question is essential to any further moves towards European integration. In the third chapter of this book I quoted from the noble preamble of the European Convention on Human Rights which to me is the most fundamental statement of the basic rights of European citizens. This statement is as clear and basic as the original Declaration of Independence of the United States and does not require any extra embellishment. Furthermore, since the signatories to the Convention have ratified this document, everyone's basic rights were clearly laid down before the European Community was ever thought of. Thus, for citizens of EC Member States the only question we need to ask ourselves is to what degree the Community Treaties enhance or detract from this Convention. This point we shall return to later in this chapter since questions of citizenship and migration require our more immediate attention.

EUROPEAN CITIZENSHIP

According to the Treaty on European Union, nationals of EC Member States are automatically considered as being European citizens. This definition is both clear and nebulous because it does not take account of the fact that different Member States do have different criteria for citizenship and it also leaves outside the pale those migrants or visitors who may clearly be Europeans but not nationals of EC Member States. This is an unacceptable state of affairs. It is, nevertheless, useful to examine the ways in which one may become a citizen of a country in Western Europe. These are:

1. At least one of the parents must be a citizen of that country.
2. One must be born in the country in question, though, where the parents do not hold citizenship, the child when he or she reaches his/her majority is required to elect for citizenship of the country of birth or his parents' citizenship – though some countries allow dual citizenship.
3. One may acquire citizenship through naturalization.
4. Through marriage.

The majority of West European countries would accept any of these criteria for citizenship, but the one major exception is Germany. Whilst Germany has, until recently at least, had the most liberal asylum laws, she does not grant citizenship easily – in a decade it granted the same number as France did in one year. Thus, practically all the children born in Germany to Turkish parents are classified as Turks. In contrast, inhabitants of the Volga region of Russia whose German ancestors settled there centuries ago may claim German citizenship as a matter of right. More recently, France, whilst not adopting the rigid German stance on citizenship, has stated, in the person of Charles Pasqua, the Minister of the Interior, that being born in France (of non–French parents, of course) does not automatically confer the right of citizenship on an individual. Regarding the fourth point on my list, both Britain and France are highly suspicious of marriages of convenience as a possible means of acquiring citizenship.

But, if we can establish that we are citizens of a Member State of the European Community or of EFTA (to limit, for the moment, discussion to Western Europe), then, what are our rights? At the outset, I would say that we must have fundamental rights to a decent education and health. But, all our rights are, in fact, laid down in the European Convention on Human Rights. Not suprisingly, our Irish friends have made the most striking use of this facility. Thus, for example, an erudite and gay Irish Senator got his friend Mary Robinson (now President of Ireland) to take his demand for the right to lead his private life as he wished to Strasburg – and he won.

MIGRATION AND ASYLUM RIGHTS

In the same week both *Le Monde*[1] and the *Guardian*[2] published articles about a policy of 'Fortress Europe' regarding migration. In the *Le Monde* article Charles Pasqua, the French Minister of the Interior, talked about a policy of 'zero migration'. Clearly, in a time of high unemployment migrants do become the scapegoats for citizens of EC Member States who themselves feel victimized. In reality, however, there are fewer legal migrants in Western Europe [3] than is believed by most people. Furthermore, as far as Western Europe is concerned, most migrants are dynamic people who undertake jobs which we do not want to do. Then, as the National Statistical Institute (INSEE) in Paris recently pointed out, in France, a country like Germany of relatively low birth rates, migrants have higher rates. The real problem with the legal migrants is that they tend to concentrate in certain metropolitan areas. Then, in comparison with former migrants from Poland and more recent ones from Portugal, they do not integrate easily into the receiving societies. More dynamic social and educational policies could help to remedy this problem. Having said this, it is clear that Western Europe gains from migrants and selective migration should be encouraged.

Turning to the question of asylum, we learn about chilling developments both inside the Community and at a Pan-European level. Although one can understand the German dilemma since they have been flooded with asylum seekers, the more Pan-European Dublin Convention of 1990 was in fact enacted before the German situation became acute. When I asked Monica den Boer about this Convention, she gave me the following information:[4]

> The Dublin Convention is, strictly spoken, not a European Community Convention, but an intergovernmental convention (or 'paracommunitarian' as some prefer to call it) between the EC Member

States. The full title of the Convention is 'Convention Determining the State Responsible for Examining Applications for Asylum Lodged in one of the Member States of the EC'. The Convention was signed on June 15, 1990, in Dublin, and has now been ratified by six of the twelve Member States (as you can see from your Agence Europe newletter). It provided that each asylum request should be handled by only one Member State, and thereby ended the so-called 'orbiting' of refugees to another Member State. Cynics say that it ought to prevent asylum-seekers from 'asylum-shopping', once refused by the one Member State, one could go to another one. This is now not possible anymore. It will in the future become even more difficult when asylum applications and refusals will be centrally registered, for example by means of the planned European Information System. There is also talk about an EC-wide introduction of a fingerprint-system for refugees.

den Boer, 1990

When I myself examined this document, having waded through the turgid legalistic mumbo-jumbo, I realied that it was just a dreadful exercise in passing the buck.

John Carvel's article in the *Guardian* on migration and asylum makes frightening reading indeed.[5] In reference to a leaked document, he talks of a chillingly named 'Expulsion Sub-Group of the Ad Hoc Group on Immigration'! Quite simply, the aim is the internal policing of migrants by groups of faceless, nameless civil servants. We are all in deep trouble and these developments are a negation of all we fought for in World War II. A more recent and extremely detailed and erudite study, edited by Tony Bunyan, gives a disturbing insight into the development of semi-official committees and other bodies inside the EC for controlling citizens, which, in most cases, have no responsibility to either the national parliaments or the European Parliament.

As can be seen in the EC's Social Charter, the basic rights of workers inside the Community are clearly laid down. At a more Pan-European level, the fundamental human rights of citizens in the 32 signatory countries of the European Convention on Human Rights are quite explicit. Thus, whenever a worker who is not a national of an EC Member State – but is a national of a country which has signed the European Convention on Human Rights – should clearly enjoy the rights as laid down in the Convention when migrating to the Community. Consequently, I am sure that the anti-migration moves inside the EC which have been examined in this chapter are quite contrary to this Convention.

In order to help safeguard the rights of European citizens I would make the following proposals:

(i)   The concept of European citizenship should be more widely defined.

(ii) The European Community should take the European Convention on Human Rights as its Constitution on Citizens' Rights.

(iii) The Community should adopt a policy of actively encouraging a policy of selective migration.

(iv) All migrants should enjoy the same social rights as those enjoyed by citizens of EC Member States.

(v)   Ad hoc groups for internal policing should be abolished.

NOTES

1. *Le Monde*, Editorial, 'L'Europe Forteresse', 3 June 1993.
2. The *Guardian*, John Carvel, 'Fortress Europe Prepares to Wall in Its Racism', 27 May 1993.
3. They constitute only about 5 per cent of the total EC population.
4. Dublin Convention, 15 June 1990, Convention Determining the State Responsibility for Examining Applications for Asylum Lodged in One of the Member States of the European Communities.
5. John Carvel, op. cit.
6. Tony Bunyan, editor, *Statewatching the New Europe*, Statewatch, Nottingham, 1993.

14. Conclusions:
What the Future might Bring

It is no platitude when we say that Europe finds itself at the most historic and challenging crossroads since 1945. Never before did we have such a great need of men with vision and determination. Alas, apart from Jacques Delors, President of the Commission of the European Communities, I do not see any politician who displays these necessary qualities. Indeed, in January, this year, the *Financial Times* talked of 'men without vision with nowhere to go'. In a similar article at about the same time, *Le Monde* echoed these views. Therefore, we have to ask ourselves, where are we likely to be going and where should we go?

As I observed earlier in this book, we have solid achievements on record. The European Community, which does, however, not constitute the whole of Europe, has practically achieved its common market as embodied in the Single European Act. Then, in the signing of the agreement between the Community and EFTA, which will lead to the creation of the European Economic Area (EEA), we shall have created the world's most sophisticated and integrated trading area. These are notable achievements.

Europe is integrating still further, and, whether we like it or not, we have to face a number of issues of immediate importance. The issues which are already upon us and which require immediate and ongoing action are the enlargement of the Community and institutional reforms, economic and monetary policies, foreign and military policies, the position of Germany and the rights of citizens in European countries. Inevitably, as I have tried to explain earlier in this work, it will be mainly our internal economic policies – rather than official foreign policy statements – which will influence the evolution of a common foreign policy. This may, nevertheless, change in the twenty-first century.

THE ENLARGEMENT OF THE COMMUNITY AND INSTITUTIONAL REFORMS

The Community has laid down absolutely clearly four criteria which possible future members of the EC must first meet. The four current applicants clearly meet these criteria and the difficult part of the negotiations between them and the Community are about to begin. They are all fairly wealthy countries but there exist areas of contention between the two sides, notably, agricultural policy, fisheries (in the case of Norway), policies for the Arctic and sub-Arctic regions (in the cases of the Scandinavian countries) and the state monopoly for alcohol in the case of Sweden. One common feature of all these states is their policy of neutrality. This could cause problems if the Community is really serious about having a common security policy. These difficulties can, however, be overcome if Member States continue to remain completely free (as will almost certainly be the case) to join or not to join NATO. Should they desire (voluntarily, of course) a greater degree of European military co-operation, they would always be free to join the WEU.

But all new Member States must accept the Treaty of Rome, the Treaty on European Union (which supersedes the Single European Act) and the intervening *acquis communautaires*. All this, despite the fears of President Mitterand, implies a deepening of the Community, but it also makes it more difficult for other countries to join the EC. Therefore, I believe it will be extremely difficult for Eastern European countries to join the Community before well into the next century. In the meantime, generous special arrangements should be made for these countries.

All this means that there is a growing urgency for the reform of the Community's institutions. Here, I foresee the practical and urgent necessity of making such reforms which will compel the present and future EC Member States to compromise. As the Community integrates still further, it will also become even more imperative to make still deeper institutional reforms as proposed by Alan Sked.

Certainly, the present lack of accountability and relative lack of democracy in these institutions makes reform indispensable. Thus, I foresee reforms in the roles of the Commission, the Council of Ministers, the Parliament and the Court of Justice. In the immediate future, I believe that the number of Commissioners will be drastically reduced.

ECONOMIC AND MONETARY POLICIES

The débâcle of the Exchange Rate Mechanism (ERM) of the European Monetary System (EMS), present levels of unemployment and doubts about Europe's international competitive position mean that decisions about our economic and monetary policies must and will be taken as a matter of urgent necessity.

At the outset, however, it should be stressed that the EC and EFTA Member States are, for the most part, highly developed countries with advanced systems of education, well-trained workers and very advanced technology. Consequently, it seems to be the misuse of these assets rather than their non-existence which is the real problem facing us at the present time. Consequently, we should adopt the following strategy if we are to fully utilize our human and technological resources:

(i) Where possible, we should improve our educational systems. An optimum type of educational package would be a combination of the Belgian and German high school systems— which combine breadth with depth; the British tutorial-based university education system, and a combination of the French and German apprenticeship and training systems. Certainly, where young people do not go on to advanced university-type education, they should have access to training or apprenticeship schemes.

(ii) Most observers are now in agreement that the present social security systems, which are too automatic and generous in some countries, need reforming. The savings made through these reforms could be channelled into employment-creating projects.

(iii)Then, we need to compensate achievement, which in some EC and
     EFTA Member States is sadly lacking.

Whilst I do not believe that these three groups of reforms will
constitute the total panacea for all our economic woes, I do believe that
they are the strictest minimum set of requirements which we must meet
if we are to use the talents of Europeans fully. They would have to be
complemented by the application of a dynamic competition policy
inside the whole of the EEA. Without this, we are likely to see a
continuation of the present increase in protective mergers between
enterprises inside the EC – thus negating the dynamic effects of the
Single European Market. Equally, we have to take decisions about the
future evolution of the Community's economic and monetary union
(EMU).

So much has been and continues to be written about the EC's
attempts at creating an economic and monetary union and our
disastrous experience with the EMS over the past year that I fear that
everyone is bewildered and lost. Therefore, I shall restrict myself to a
few basic facts which I believe have been overlooked. Once we are
clear about basic principles and possibilities, the Community and
perhaps some EFTA states will, I believe, be able to move along the
road – but at different speeds for different countries – towards
achieving an EMU.

First, the EC Member States are 'open' or 'very open' economies
which are conducting 60 per cent of their trade with each other. This
means that they demand each others' currencies for trading purposes.
However, some countries are very much more open than others and are
consequently more integrated with one or all EC trading partners. This
is particularly the case of the Netherlands *vis-à-vis* Germany. With or
without this 'openness', internal economic conditions (e.g. levels of
inflation and budgetary deficits) must not differ too much since this will
inevitably lead to the use of interest rate differentials which will cause
tensions in the system – witness, for example, the cases of Belgium and
Germany. These tensions will cause problems for countries whose

economies are strong, e.g. France. All this implies that if EC Member States are serious about having an EMU then they must co-ordinate their policies as was apparently their intention following the conclusion of the Nyborg/Basel Agreements in 1987. Equally, they *must* adhere to the four policy steps as laid down at the end of 1978 for participating countries whose currencies come under pressure on the exchange markets.

Naturally, as countries move closer to creating a full EMU, they will gradually lose more of their freedom to adjust exchange rates and to take internal policy decisions. Thus, there will be an even greater need for compensating funds. Although a major increase in the resources of the EC's Regional and Social Funds took place between 1989 and 1993, and a further increase is underway for the coming four or five years, these resources are unlikely to be adequate. Furthermore, any further increases will be increasingly unacceptable for such contributors as Britain, Germany and the Netherlands. As if this is not enough, some future EC Member States – the Scandinavian and Eastern European ones – will bring major regional problems with them.

Finally, I do not consider that it will be easy to achieve an EMU unless we are trading a much greater degree of our GDP (say 70 per cent) among ourselves – together with the application of correct internal policies. This implies that for the foreseeable future we shall have to live with a Community with Member States moving towards an EMU at different speeds.

And, what about the control of capital movements and a future European currency? Regarding the former question, there have always existed clauses in Community legislation enabling Member States to introduce capital and exchange controls whenever their currencies come under pressure on the exchange markets. At the present time such a respite may last for up to 180 days – though I am sure that this period could be extended. Last year, both Ireland and Spain availed themselves of this safeguard clause in order to protect their currencies. More recently, Jacques Delors called for the introduction of new measures to control capital movements. Whilst I understand President Delors' attitude – particularly when the currency of the strongest economy of the EC, that of France, has been under constant and repeated pressure – I believe that any such measures would have to be the result of an international agreement and could hardly be undertaken by the EC alone. Since, however, much of the recent speculation has been undertaken by highly 'respectable' organizations, such as pension funds and insurance funds, then these bodies would have to have their legal rights to speculate restricted. One may well imagine the uproar which any such moves by the EC may occasion. If the Community is really serious about achieving a full EMU – even on an à la carte basis, then the best way to resist speculation is to co-ordinate their economic and monetary policies – including interest rate differentials. As has already been mentioned, the resulting loss of sovereignty will necessitate the provision of generous financial compensation – and that is another matter altogether – but will be much cheaper than the fabulous amounts of cash lost by central banks in 1992-93 in trying to prop up their currencies on the exchange markets. To date, no central banker and no finance minister has been brought to account for these losses. Such behaviour would never be tolerated in the business world.

And a European currency? Some say we have two at the present time – the DM and the ECU. The DM is heavily used for trading, investment and speculative purposes whilst the ECU is the official unit of the EC as well as being the numéraire of the ERM of the EMS. The commercial ECU has, in recent years, been increasingly used for trading and safety purposes because of its great inherent quality as a 'risk spreader'.

Despite my own desire for a European currency which will reflect the great economic and commercial power of the Community, I do not (whatever is said in the Treaty on European Union) possibly foresee such a development in the foreseeable future. Instead, as all or just some of the EC Member States become more integrated, then there may be a legitimate and an increasing need for a European currency. Should the German economy increasingly dominate the EC, then the common currency for general purposes will continue to be the DM whilst the ECU will be used for official purposes. Imagine, however, that there is a more balanced development among the Member States, then it would be more likely that the common currency for trade purposes would be the ECU. However, even if this development takes place, for practical, psychological and physical reasons, the ECU would not be the unique currency. Rather, there would be a group of parallel currencies, the ECU and the national currencies of the EC Member States.

FOREIGN AND MILITARY POLICIES

As the world's greatest trading bloc – with its power about to be enhanced by the creation of the EEA – the Community is indeed in an enviable international position. In the successive rounds of Multilateral Trade Negotiations (MTNs), organized in the framework of the GATT, the EC, ever since the Kennedy Round, has, together with the United States, been the chief negotiating bloc and protagonist. As with the United States, many countries desire to have privileged trading relations with the EC. Thus, the recent threat by France to veto the agreement made with the United States in November 1992 in the area of agricultural policy (thus jeopardizing the successful outcome of the Uruguay Round) is extremely worrying. Personally, I cannot believe that France will go the whole way and upset the world's trading system, but we shall see.

In the area of foreign policy, I think that the EC's main area of activity will be trade where there are many policy possibilities. But, there is and will continue to be one major change at the diplomatic level. This change is the new diplomatic role of Germany for which the Community seems to be quite unprepared. The position of Germany will be discussed in detail later in this chapter. At this point it is enough to say that this change is causing and will increasingly lead to tensions between France and Germany. Consequently, however discreetly it is done, I foresee an active revival of the presently dormant *entente cordiale* between France and Britain. Wisely, Britain is not trying to come between France and Germany at the present time. Thus, apart from this ongoing change, I consider that the overwhelming part of the Community's foreign policy will be restricted to trade for the foreseeable future.

In contrast, military policy is and will become more dynamic. Here, I have stressed the urgent necessity of substantially increasing the size of NATO's Rapid Deployment Force (RDF) because most recent military conflicts have been and are increasingly likely to take place in Europe. As a consequence of these needs, I see a more dynamic role for the WEU.

Although the planned joint Franco-German Military Corps (with a possible participation by Belgium and Spain) is a laudable move, I believe it to be more symbolic than real because no one knows precisely how it will function. Fortunately, more recently, France and Germany have agreed to link it with the WEU and with NATO. In any case, this corps will not come on stream for some time yet – hence the most urgent need of increasing NATO's RDF.

This brings us to the question of NATO membership for Eastern European countries. This is a complicated issue, since, logically, Russia has to accept such moves. Following the publication in *Le Monde*, in August 1992, of a report that Russia (apparently) had no objection to Poland's membership of NATO, things could be changing. Such a move would constitute a revolution in European history and we must be absolutely sure of the situation in advance in view of NATO's motto to interpret an attack on one member as an attack on all. We must not mislead Eastern European countries with false hopes (as we have done so much in the past). In the meantime, Franco-British policies on common procurement in the military field and joint nuclear (military) co-operation are positive and should be intensified.

THE POSITION OF GERMANY

It seems that most observers have been so stunned by the unification of the two Germanies that they dare not look into the future – and yet, look we must! As in the past, in the position and in the behaviour of Germany lies the future of Europe. Until now, the 1963 Treaty of Co-operation between France and the then Federal Republic of Germany (or West Germany) and West Germany's membership of the EC, NATO, WEU and the Council of Europe had secured her to the West. Furthermore, despite the integration of most of the judges and other legal hacks, who had served the Nazis so diligently, into the legal apparatus of the Federal Republic, West Germany has been a model democracy. Now, unspoken fears among citizens in Eastern and Western Europe suggest that all this may change. What, then, might happen, and what should we do?

First, absolutely without the benefit of hindsight, I can say that in 1990[1] I warned about the present troubles which unification would occasion. Similarly, I warned about an artificial conversion of East Marks into Deutsche Marks and I calculated that German unification would cost much more than the naive figures being put forward then. As a result of this (though I did not forecast the massive migration into Germany from the East and from the ex-Yugoslavia), I suggested that massive aid would be needed – both from Germany itself as well as from the rest of the EC. Personally, I believe that this Community solidarity is more necessary than ever before. I shall return to this theme later in this section.

The unification of the two Germanies does then, apart from all the other current challenges, present Europe with its greatest challenge and opportunity in decades. This unification has made Germany the most populous country in the EC and it was already the strongest in economic terms. Although the unification, economically speaking, has been badly handled, and although social, psychological *and* linguistic differences between the two Germanies will remain for decades to come, I think it possible that within 10 to 15 years the two Germanies will have been firmly integrated together economically.

Historically, there has, at all times – even before the time of Peter the Great – been an inevitable and usually fatal mutual attraction between Germany and the countries of Central and Eastern Europe. Whilst the fatal part of the relationship has now disappeared, the mutual attraction remains. Even before the fall of the Berlin Wall, West Germany conducted more trade with Eastern and Central Europe than any other EC country and had important investments in those parts of Europe. The interests have increased and will continue to increase. Consequently, whilst Germany is not at all militarist in nature, she will, logically, demand a bigger say in European and world affairs. The first sign of this is her demand for a permanent place on the UN Security Council. This will make the Franco-German relationship much more one-sided and will cause the French to reinvigorate the dormant Franco-British *entente cordiale*.

What, then, should the rest of the Community do? It is still not too late to help with the unification of the two Germanies. This can be done in two ways. First, much greater help should be given to Germany in dealing with the massive influx of refugees. More specifically, all EC Member States should take in more of these refugees from Germany. Second, at a Community level, far more substantial funds should be given to Germany to help with the renewal of the infrastructure in the former East Germany. After all, since the division of Germany was not a purely German affair, so the reunification is also not an exclusively national affair.

Regarding Britain, a gesture is surely urgently needed for the inexcusable and criminal bombing of Dresden in 1945 and the equally incomprehensible unveiling of a statue, last year, in London, to the chief perpetrator of this crime, 'Bomber' Harris. I would most strongly advise the British Government to send substantial donations to the fund set up for the reconstruction of the Frauenkirche, in Dresden.

Inevitably, Germany, with its highly educated and trained workforce and its important investments in Central and Eastern Europe, is set to become, within a few years, the most important economic power in Europe. Consequently, within the next ten years, Berlin will become Europe's political and cultural capital.

THE RIGHTS OF CITIZENS IN EUROPEAN COUNTRIES

The 40th anniversary of the coming into force of the European Convention on Human Rights occured on 3 September, 1993. In a particularly pertinent article in the *Financial Times* earlier that year, Anthony Lester [2] highlighted the inexorable growth in the membership of the Council of Europe and the recent acceptance by Hungary, Poland and the Czech Republic of the right of individual petition (by their citizens) under the convention. He also referred to the ever-increasing time it takes between the moment when an individual complains to Strasburg and when the Court gives judgement. Consequently, he welcomes the plan, supported by two-thirds of the Member States of the Council of Europe (including France and Germany) to create a single full-time European Court of Justice which would replace the present cumbersome two-tier system. In contrast, he strongly criticizes Britain's attempts to prevent this reform in favour of a change in the present two-tier system proposed by the Netherlands and Sweden. Personally, I cannot imagine what Britain has to fear from a full-time permanent European Court of Justice. After all, Britain's laws on racism are second to none and we do have strong equal rights legislation. No, as Anthony Lester has advocated, Britain should be in the vanguard of European countries calling for reform. This is particularly important since the Council of Europe is the one parliamentary organization where countries from all parts of Europe can meet. Then, without wishing to bore readers, the European Convention on Human Rights is *the* statement, clearly written, of the basic rights of all citizens in all countries which are signatories to it. It is such an important document that I feel that all citizens in the signatory countries should receive a copy. In comparison with the United States, for example, Western European countries do guarantee (financially) the rights of their citizens to education and health. In the field of health, Britain, Denmark and Ireland organize a transfer of resources, via the national budget, from the richer to the poorer sections of the community. However, in other fields concerning the rights of citizens, the situation is less rosy and gives cause for very grave concern.

The written statement made by Monica Den Boer about formal and 'informal' police controls over migrants makes chilling reading. What would prevent these controls from being extended to other citizens? The recent spate of criminal miscarriages of justice in Britain do nothing to reassure us. It is no wonder then that Denmark, the one country (apart from Bulgaria) in occupied Europe during World War II which deliberately saved its Jewish citizens, wants no truck with all this. Indeed, Denmark should be our humane model for the European Community. I shall return to this point in a moment.

Without wishing to indulge in self-righteousness, the rise of racism in France, Germany and the Netherlands is inexcusable. Although I do not expect the present state of affairs to be changed overnight, at least, in the case of Germany, the basic human rights of the Turks and their right to citizenship should and could be guaranteed very quickly.

Returning to Denmark, here is a country of freedom where couples, whatever their sexual persuasion, can become legally linked together. In contrast, England (though not Scotland) seems to be still living in the Middle Ages. Thus, I would promote Denmark as the model which not only the EC Member States but also all signatories to the European Convention on Human Rights should emulate.

NEW CHALLENGES

Recently, the bringing together of ten of the Commonwealth of Independent States (CIS) into a loose form of economic union (perhaps, eventually, like the former European Payments Union, EPU, in Western Europe?) heralds a new form of challenge to Western Europe. The coming together of former Soviet Republics is logical since they were formerly so inextricably linked together economically (as well as in other ways) with Russia – who was their main supplier of energy. Where are they to find a replacement for such a massive supplier and such a captive market?

More ominous, however, is Russia's renewed ambition (the origins of which go back to the westward thrust of Muscovy which predate Peter the Great) in the military field and the unspoken but apparent desire to recreate a Greater Russia. This development certainly places NATO in a much greater dilemma regarding possible membership for Central and Eastern European countries, which, to me, can only be contemplated if we are both able and willing, as has hitherto been the case, to come to the defence of any NATO Member State which comes under attack. In the specific case of NATO itself, we could not afford to emulate the West's military self-castration which we witnessed in Hungary in 1956 and Czechoslovakia in 1968.

Ideally, it is desirable to associate, as much as possible, the countries of Central and Eastern Europe and the former Soviet Union with NATO. Currently, this is being done through the work of NATO's Co-operation Council. This body includes all the Member States of the now dead Warsaw Pact. However, we have to temper our optimism with caution and realism and we must never again mislead countries as we did with Hungary, in 1956, and, more recently, the parts of the former Yugoslavia. We do not know (though we can hazard an intelligent guess) which way the new Greater Russia will turn – especially now that it is taking control of the Ukraine's atomic warheads and Black Sea fleet (however outdated). No, we have to keep our powder dry and should make the following reaffirmations and take the following steps:

(i) Reaffirm NATO's original pledge and motto, 'One for all, all for one'.
(ii) Only admit new members to which this pledge can be realistically extended.
(iii) Rapidly increase the size of the Rapid Deployment Force.
(iv) Accelerate moves towards common procurement. Here, already existing Franco-British joint procurement and production should be increased. More important still, the rationalization by WEU's Western European Armaments Group (WEAG) should be accelerated. This will enable the RDF to be equipped more quickly.
(v) Finally, much more money should be devoted to the work of NATO's Co-operation Council thus accelerating the sharing of NATO's co-operation policies – under civilian control – with the countries of the former Warsaw Pact.

Although the adoption of these five measures will do much to help us to face the future with a greater degree of equanimity, we should in no way tamper with the Franco-British nuclear deterrent since we can never be sure which way the storms will blow in future years.

OPTIMISM AND/OR PESSIMISM

In spite of the fears I have just expressed about the rights of citizens in EC Member States – and developments in the CIS, I tend to be more optimistic (but then, that is my basic nature) than pessimistic about the future of Europe. What are the grounds for my optimism?

At the political level, I am thrilled by the political clean-up in Italy. The Italians have faced the political corruption head-on and have had the courage to reform their constitution and reinforce their tired democracy. Of at least equal importance is their battle against the very dangerous members of the Mafia. These are brave acts and the Italian people are reinforcing democracy in Europe.

Similarly, the collapse of Communism and the revival of democracy in Central and Eastern Europe constitute a positive revolution. But, if democracies are not only to survive but to be reinforced, we must provide more help and encouragement to those countries.

Of equal importance is disarmament. This equally great revolution releases scarce technological resources for peacetime use. Here, however, we need to replace the more conventional forces with a much larger high quality RDF.

And, economically speaking, will Europe be competitive in future years? Apart from anything else, we (like the Japanese) are an ageing population and must therefore use our scarce resources in an optimum manner whilst adopting a policy of 'product differentiation'. Here, I find two reasons for moderate optimism.

First, acceptance by the EC Council of Ministers, in June, last year, of nearly all the revolutionary proposals contained in Ray MacSharry's paper[3] on the reform of the CAP, was proof of an important change in EC policies regarding an improved allocation of resources. Second, in an interesting study,[4] the joint editors, Alexis Jacquemin and David Wright, noted an increasing concern in EC Member States with education and training:

> There is also a broad-based consensus among the Institutes that education and training will be important shaping factor components of successful economies in the 1990s and beyond, as well as long-term response to some forms of unemployment. The French paper says endogenous human capital will be a crucial component of growth whether it be R&D policy and practice, education or demographic change. The education – training – information triplet could transform economic activity in the decades ahead they suggest. Likewise, technology and the ability to absorb technological change feature stongly across the board, with much

emphasis placed on the growing ease of technology and diffusion, the information networks and the speed of information flows as a means of generating greater economic flexibility in a growing interdependent world.

Jacquemin and Wright, 1993

My only concern is that we might not reform education and training sufficiently quickly.

In view of my concern with the rights of European citizens it would be wrong not to give some place to the EC's Social Charter and the inclusion of the Charter's main tenets in the Treaty on European Union. I believe that the Social Chapter is a noble document which lays down the basic rights of workers. However, like Mrs. Thatcher, I believe that any attempts at laying down a minimum guaranteed European wage would lead us to economic catastrophe – similar to that experienced by the former East Germany as attempts have been made to equalize wages in the two Germanies. In contrast, I consider that German moves to spread worker consultation and participation throughout the EC to be a basic right and a successful means of removing the 'them and us' attitude in Britain.

And, a United States of Europe? No, certainly not. Because of our differences in traditions, tastes and in integration, we shall have a Europe à la carte for the foreseeable future. Although I myself would like to see more integration, I think the present situation of a multi-speed Europe to be both healthy and logical. In the long run, however, as we integrate still further we can expect more common foreign policy decisions to be taken. Also, we can expect to see the use of a common European currency and national currencies alongside each other. Politically speaking, rather than a United States of Europe, I think we can expect to see the creation of a European Confederation. As in the past, we can expect to have pleasant (as well as unpleasant) surprises which will encourage EC Member States to move closer together more quickly. The best example here is the defeat in the French Parliament of the European Defence Treaty, which, indirectly, led to the creation of the EEC. The future will be full of surprises.

Finally, I do believe that we can solve so many of our regional and political differences in the framework of the European Community.

Thus, as EC Member States Britain and Ireland – despite the cruel and inexcusable terrorism – have made much progress in solving the Northern Ireland problem. The acceptance by Mrs. Thatcher of Ireland's right of consultation in policy decisions concerning Northern Ireland was a revolutionary achievement. It is doubtful whether this could have been achieved without the umbrella of the Community. Similarly, other regional problems in France and Spain, for example, will be solved under the same umbrella.

Despite my criticism of the Treaty on European Union and my fears about a possible misuse of the right of veto in the EC Council of Ministers which originated in the so-called Luxemburg Compromise of 1966,[5] the Treaty does contain two provisions which bode well for the future and which contradict some of my earlier criticisms. One development is the creation of a Committee of the Regions which has the potential, in the long run, of giving power to hitherto neglected regions. The other is the creation of an Ombudsman in the framework of the European Parliament – with right of petition by citizens of EC Member States. Potentially, this is a wonderful development in the field of human rights. Our task will now be to give the European Parliament the necessary teeth by adopting the proposals made by Alan Sked in his constructive paper, 'Proposal for a European Union'.

POSSIBLE FUTURE TENSIONS AND DEVELOPMENTS – A SUPPLEMENT

The major part of the work, up to this point in my book, had been completed in the summer of 1993. Fortunately my publisher was kind enough to allow me to write this supplement in October. We both felt that it was both desirable and necessary to examine certain important developments which occurred since the completion of the main part of the manuscript.

Obviously, the most important development was the acceptance by Germany's Constitutional Court of the Treaty on European Union. Consequently, this Treaty becomes law inside the European Community in November 1993. This decision revives all the discussion about an economic and monetary union (EMU) and an eventual political union (PU) among the Member States.

Although the major upheavals that have continued in the currency markets with varying degrees of ferocity since the summer of 1992 are clearly visible even to a non-expert, and, despite important political changes in all parts of Europe, discussions about a future EMU and a possible PU continue as though nothing had happened! Thus even though I did not want to write anything more about these topics – believing brevity is a virtue – I feel obliged to join in the discussion.

We are told that the EMU[6] is still on course! In the same breath, we learn that the Bundesbank is still sticking to its fundamental tenet that control of M3 is and will continue to be the basis of its monetary policy. Consequently, it is implied that if other EC Member States, other than the Netherlands, also wish to join in an EMU, they are 'invited' to accept this tenet of the Bundesbank.[7] The experience of other countries in the West which use 'inflationary targets' is, it seems, ignored by the directors of the German Central Bank. This behaviour is, to say the least, extremely disquieting and incomprehensible, since most economists would agree that the control of inflation involves a judicious use of both fiscal and monetary policies. Indeed, Donald MacDougall, in his famous report, published in 1977,[8] stressed the increasingly important role which fiscal policy will play in a European Economic Community which wishes to integrate still further – possibly leading to 'pre-federal or small or large federal' sectors. More recently, in a different but related study,[9] he has stressed, once again, the importance of the role of fiscal policy in the integration process.

All this implies the existence of a great deal of co-ordination between the finance ministries and central banks of the EC Member States, the Council of Ministers and the Commission. The strictest minimum of co-operation we need is a respect of the four policy steps which have to be taken by ERM members when their national currencies come under pressure. Equally, an activation of the moribound Basel/Nyborg Agreement on policy co-ordination is indispensable. Eventually, as the Commission has always suggested, if countries are serious about an EMU, they would pool their reserves of gold and foreign currencies – a proposal which does not appeal to all countries – especially the Bundesbank.

Discussion about the strict criteria which Member States must fulfill if they wish to enter the final stage of an EMU – as laid down in the Treaty on European Union – seem to be almost pointless since only Luxemburg meets these requirements!   Now Luxemburg is contemplating breaking its monetary union with Belgium (concluded in 1922) because the Belgians are not keeping their economic and monetary house in order.   Already in 1982, Belgium's unilateral devaluation of the Belgian franc had raised the ire of the Luxemburgers – for the same reasons.

MY PROPOSAL FOR AN EVENTUAL EMU

Without wishing to repeat myself in a seemingly endless manner, I would lay down the following criteria for links between national currencies and the creation of an EMU:

(i)   countries link their currencies together because they conduct trade with each other, thus,

(ii)   as all economists will agree, small very open economies will link their currencies extremely closely with their major trading partner(s). Consequently, the former close links between the Irish Punt and the Pound Sterling (which did, in fact, amount to a *de facto* monetary union) were both logical and desirable. At the present time, the same applies to the links between the German and Dutch currencies.

(iii) An EMU, however, does imply a high degree of integration. Thus, as already referred to in Chapter 6, the United States, whilst not perhaps constituting an ideal optimum currency area (OCA), does, because it conducts about 90 per cent of its trade with itself, constitute an excellent EMU. Logically, then, the EC Member States would have to be much more open (with some exceptions) to each other than they are at the present time.

(iv)   Equally, good economic and monetary housekeeping is necessary among countries forming an EMU among themselves. If some are borrowing too much on the capital markets (and sometimes for long periods of time) they could 'crowd out' others and this behaviour is therefore not acceptable. Likewise, they cannot be favouring their own institutions and enterprises at the expense of their neighbours. A great degree of economic and monetary co-ordination then becomes a necessity.

(v) As already mentioned, in the domain of policy co-ordination, I would propose the use of inflationary targets – supported by a judicious use of fiscal and monetary policies. Countries which suceed in achieving their targets could be rewarded in some way.

(vi) As already discussed in Chapter 9, further moves towards a greater degree of integration will certainly require the use of a much more active regional policy than is presently the case.

(vii) If and when EC Member States decide to fully support each others' currencies, then a pooling of reserves should be contemplated.

(viii) For the foreseeable future, and in the absence of a respect of the four policy steps for active members of the ERM, the present wide bands of fluctuation around the parities of the participating currencies of the EMS are the only practical policy.

(ix) The question of a common currency is more problematical. The decision of the Council meeting in Brussels, on 29 October 1993, to create a common currency by the end of 1999 was incomprehensible to say the least. In the absence of a firm and active programme of policy co-ordination this decision was both childish and dangerous. If, however, we are going to have a common currency, in order to save what remains of the professionalism of politicians and technocrats, then it can only be a parallel or 'hard' currency alongside the national currencies of the EC Member States.

(x) All these criteria imply that *par la force des choses* all Western countries will integrate at different speeds. Consequently, some countries will, at different stages over time, be stronger candidates than others for an EMU. At the Community or EEA level, the points I raised in (iii) are very relevant and critical. If we ignore these basic economic and monetary tensions we shall discredit ourselves forever and create tensions which we shall never be able to resolve this century.

On a more positive note, frequent reference has been made to the necessity of providing financial transfers between the regions and Member States of the Community if we intend to move towards the implementation of a full EMU. Although, as has already been mentioned, the amounts of money allocated to the Regional and Social Funds will be doubled over the period 1994-99, it is necessary to do so much more at the structural level. Thus, it is reassuring to know that the EC has allocated and is activating a number of extra facilities for structural projects.

As *Europe* reported on 16 October 1993, the current situation with these facilities is as follows:

(i) of the special temporary lending facility of 5 billion ECUs (increased to 8 billion at the Copenhagen Summit) of the European Investment Bank (EIB), about 3 billion have been loaned for 46 projects which include the extension to the Jubilee Underground (metro) railway line in London and the Belgian high speed train.

(ii) In contrast, the European Investment Fund, financed by private banks (one-third of the capital) and the EIB and the EC (the other two-thirds) is not yet operational. When it comes on stream it will have 2 billion ECUs to supply credit guarantees on loans totalling 20 billion ECUs.

(iii) Fortunately, the Cohesion Fund (not to be confused with the structural Regional and Social Funds) is operational and has already injected 300 million ECUs into 21 projects in Ireland, Portugal and Spain.

Whilst these facilities do not constitute enormous amounts of finance – when compared with the wastage involved in the Community's CAP – they are clearly a step in the right direction since they are concerned with infrastructure projects which create employment and improve the quality of life in Europe.

FURTHER DEVELOPMENTS

At the aforementioned Council meeting, in Brussels, on 29 October 1993, Germany was awarded the supreme accolade for good behaviour (?!) when it was agreed that the seat of the future European Monetary Institute (which comes into being at the beginning of 1994) will be Frankfurt. This decision reinforces the position and strength of Germany in Europe for the future.

A much more positive development for the Greater Europe was the decision taken at the 40th anniversary ministerial meeting of the Council of Europe, in Vienna, earlier in October 1993, to create a supreme European Court of Human Rights. This is so important for all the 32 members[10] of the Council of Europe because it creates a great Pan-European organ to which the citizens of 32 European countries have direct access. In the long run, I would suggest that this body should indeed be the supreme court for Europe to which (in the absence of an upper house, for example, of the European Parliament) appeal could be made against the decisions of the European Court of Justice in Luxemburg. Such a development is essential not just because of the dangerous recent administrative developments inside the EC regarding migration but also because the consumer does not have strong rights at a Community level. In some European countries consumer associations have strong voices and are very active whereas, despite its admirable work, the European Consumers' Bureau, in Brussels, is not as strong as it should be.

FUTURE POLITICAL DEVELOPMENTS AND TENSIONS

At the aforementioned ministerial 40th anniversary meeting of the Council of Europe, in Vienna, President Mitterand called for the creation of a European Confederation. Almost at the same time, the United States expressed its support for the association of Central and Eastern European countries with NATO – but not for membership in the immediate future. Both these developments deserve closer examination and merit our reactions.

At the political level, we do have to ask ourselves where we want to go. Personally, I do not believe that we have asked this fundamental question but I consider it indispensable to do so at this moment in time. If we fail to do this, we shall create future misunderstandings and tensions. Thus, what are the options, realistic or otherwise, which are now open to us? Personally, I believe that there are three basic possible political options open to us – the first two are both realistic and practical, the third is more idealistic and long-term in nature. These are:

(i) The creation of a loose European Confederation centred on the Council of Europe.

(ii) The creation of a European kind of Switzerland – based on the EEA.

(iii) In the longer run, a Canadian-type European Federation.

A European Confederation

A European Confederation, centred on the Council of Europe as its supreme organ is attractive at a Pan-European level, since, at the time of writing, it would involve 32 countries. It would allow all the members to keep their present regional organizations and arrangements such as the EC, EFTA and free trade agreements between Central and Eastern European countries. Thus, these regional groups of countries could continue to integrate further among themselves at speeds convenient to them, but the common supreme organ would be the European Court of Human Rights – to which body all national parliaments would be subservient where human rights are concerned. This arrangement would be very suitable for a Europe à la carte arrangement and would involve many European countries.

A European Kind of Switzerland

In the light of the acceptance by all EC Member States of the Treaty on European Union and the coming into being of the EEA (now planned for the end of 1993 or early in 1994), there clearly exists a profound integration movement between the EC and EFTA countries. Furthermore, four EFTA countries are currently negotiating their membership of the Community. All this implies an acceptance by more countries of the tenets of the Treaties of Rome and European Union. Against this must be set the growing demands – notably in Britain and Denmark – for a greater openness on the part of the Council of Ministers and the Commission and more contact between the Community and its citizens. Thus, we already find ourselves facing the evolution of a European kind of Switzerland where the regions and the nation states keep much power to themselves but delegate other powers such as trade, foreign and defence policies to the centre. Switzerland is a good model for Europe because it unites four different cultures and keeps much political power at the local levels.

A Canadian-type European Federation

As the European countries integrate much further, it is likely that there will be calls by some countries for the creation of a loose European Federation rather like that of Canada. The advantage of this form of political and economic union is that it delegates to the centre the responsibility for foreign affairs, international trade, monetary policy and defence whilst responsibility for taxation and fiscal policy is shared between the Federal Government and the States. Also, since Canada is a bilingual State, the Anglophone and Francophone parts keep their cultural identities. In contrast with the example of Switzerland, there does not exist the constant active local participation in political life in the form of the frequent holding of a referendum. In Canada, such a practice is restricted to consultations about changes in the Constitution. On the economic side, an adoption of the Canadian model would necessitate major financial transfers between the regions.

Which Model for Europe?

Given the desirability of bringing the Central and Eastern European countries ever closer into the European family of nations, my immediate preference is for a loose confederation of European States. Such a confederation would, I believe, find immediate support among many European countries – notably by Britain, Denmark and France. In the long run, however, it is likely that some European nations will prefer a closer form of union. Their membership of an existing Confederation of European states would no longer prevent them from becoming members of a European kind of Switzerland or a loose Canadian-type Federation, because, in either case, the supreme organ where human rights are concerned would be the Council of Europe.

It is likely that those present and future EC Member States which actively support the common foreign policy and defence/security aims of the Treaty on European Union would, at a later date, opt for a European kind of Switzerland. As has already been mentioned, Switzerland with its bringing together of four different cultures and its active grass roots democracy would certainly appeal to some countries.

In the near future I believe it necessary for the EC and EFTA Member States to examine this question about their political future. In the immediate future, however, it is a matter of greatest urgency to balance national representation in the EC Commission, to make deliberations more open and to transform the composition of the European Parliament so that it is made up of representatives of EC national parliaments. In this way the present lack of involvement by citizens in the EC's activities could be rapidly changed.

THE MILITARY OPTION

As each day goes by I become more and more concerned about military matters. Not least of all I wonder whether Britain's defence cuts will allow us to defend our own country as well as meeting our Treaty obligations – notably those under the Dunkirk and Brussels Treaties— as well as our NATO obligations. Logically, joint procurement schemes such as the Anglo-French ones should help to diminish the effects of these cuts. Unfortunately, it seems that even these projects are not immune from the budgetary axe.[11]

Of at least equal concern is the increased strength and role of the military in Russia as a result of their support for Yeltsin in the October abortive coup. This probably explains the Russian policy turnabout regarding the possible NATO membership for Eastern and Central European countries. Here, the United States has clearly taken account of this change in attitude, when, in October, it persuaded European defence ministers to offer both former Soviet republics and East European countries closer co-operation with NATO – but not full membership. It is clear that we cannot, for reasons of credibility and morality, offer membership to these countries if we are either unable and/or unwilling to defend them should they be attacked.

For the time being, co-operation between NATO and the ex-Warsaw Pact countries should be intensified, the strength of the Rapid Deployment Force (RDF) of NATO should be considerably upgraded, joint procurements should be increased and the work of the WEU should be intensified. [12]

PRESENT AND FUTURE ECONOMIC CONTRADICTIONS AND TENSIONS – OTHER THAN MONETARY ONES

In his erudite study, [13] Pierre-André Buigues makes a number of pertinent findings relating to the Single European Market (SEM). On the one hand, he notes that in the EC only in Germany (mainly because of the size of the national market) do producers really take advantage of economies of scale. This observation would seem to imply that the SEM has some way to go before we begin to reap these advantages.

Unfortunately, other findings suggest that we shall increasingly face tensions and contradictions over the coming years if we are to reap the benefits associated with a large internal market like that enjoyed by Americans in their own country. [14] There are three findings which, alas, tend to support my fears:

(i) In another part of his study, Pierre-André Buigues notes that relatively small financial groups in Germany and Italy control proportionally very large areas of industry and commerce. In the former country, it is the bankers who own and control a major part of the economy whilst in the latter country a small amount of

financial groups controls a very important part of the economy.
(ii)   The high threshold level, a turnover of 5 billion ECUs, for planned mergers between companies before they become eligible for scrutiny by the EC commission is damaging to competition. There are mergers sometimes well below this level which lead to control by a few companies of important and vital areas in the economy.
(iii) Inside the EC, in anticipation of the SEM, mergers and acquisitions (many for defensive means) increased substantially between 1988 and 1991.

These developments will most likely lead to future conflicts and tensions between producers, owners and workers, and consumers inside the SEM and the future European Economic Area (EEA). Personally, in order to ensure that we really do reap the possible benefits of the SEA and EEA, i.e. improved choice and lower prices, I am in favour of lowering the turnover threshold for planned mergers which come under the scrutiny of the Commision. Likewise, the powers of the European Bureau of Consumers and Unions[15] should be strengthened.

As I am writing this supplement, there have been two developments of great importance. On 9 November 1993, at the economic trade level, an important trade agreement was signed between the EC and Russia in which the Community granted trade concessions to the Russians with the understanding that the Treaty would eventually lead to the signing of a free trade agreement between the two parties. This is a positive evolution between the two partners at a time when the Community has been accusing Russia of dumping aluminium on its internal market. The question one must ask is whether the Russians will be able to use such trade agreements to their advantage. I see no clear answer to this question at present. A little over a week earlier, at the political level, the French and German Heads of State and Government made (according to *Europe*, dated 29 October 1993) the following proposal to the Belgian Prime Minister, Jean-Luc Dehaene:

In order to improve the effectiveness of the Community's work, maintain the political impetus given by the European Council and stimulate closer cooperation between the national governments and the Community institutions, we also propose that the Council meet regularly at the level of Ministers, Ministers' Delegates or Secretaries of State for European Affairs, between meetings of the Foreign Ministers.

Dehaene, 1993

In an interview with the newspaper, *Le Figaro*, the French Prime Minister, Edouard Balladur, further elucidated this message when he said:

We must decide to hold councils of Ministers for European Affairs more frequently and regularly, at least twice a month, on a fixed date and to invite the Commission to submit detailed reports on its activities of the preceding two-week period and to receive necessary instructions.

Balladur, 1993

Furthermore, he added that, 'The Commission should not hold political power in the European Community. The states should.' This policy statement falls into line with proposals made (see Chapter 2) by President de Gaulle for a 'Europe of the Nation States'. The difference is that the Germans now share this view. Although Britain (at the time of writing) has not yet reacted to these proposals, I have every reason to believe that the British will support this move. The next logical step in the democratic process would be for the European Parliament to be composed of representatives from the parliaments of the EC Member States. Then, the European Court of Justice should be cut down to size, and, where human rights are concerned, made subservient to the European Court of Human Rights, in Strasburg.

POLITICAL COOPERATION – MORE RECENT DEVELOPMENTS

At the end of the end of the 1980s – alongside the COREPER – was set up the European Political Co-operation Committee (EPCC), composed of high ranking representatives of the twelve EC Member States. This little known body had been very active at an inter-governmental level. It has made several hundreds of proposals to the

Council of Ministers about many subjects, but especially concerning human rights and South Africa, nearly all of which have resulted in 'Declarations of Policy' by the Council. As from the beginning of this month (November 1993), this body has been merged with the COREPER (where, together with the Council, the real power lies in the Community) and should form the basis of important future research projects.

More recently, a working group on Internal and Judicial Affairs, Immigration and Asylum, has been set up and has been very active. Again, this body represents the governments of the EC Member States and makes recommendations to the Council.

Finally, as from 1 January 1994, the Foreign Policy and Security Committee (PESC) will be set up and will be composed of a representative of the government of each EC Member State (with the rank of ambassador) and will work alongside (and in the same building) as the COREPER. I can assume that the COREPER could eventually absorb this body.

All this implies that the EC is being 'de-Communitized' and is becoming more inter-governmental in the image of the de Gaulle thesis of a 'Europe of the Nation States'. Since, in the case of internal affairs and security and foreign affairs, we are dealing with new policy areas, the Council is monopolizing them – though it is co-operating, more than in the past, with the European Parliament. In these new areas of decision-making, the role of the Commission is becoming largely symbolic in nature.

Most recently, the re-emphasis on a French policy of a Europe of Nation States has been underlined by the nomination by the French Government, in November this year, of the Gaullist Pierre de Boissieur, as permanent representative to the European Communities/European Union.

A WORD OF CAUTION ABOUT OUR ECONOMIC FUTURE

Although I believe that the reform of the CAP gives us grounds for optimism about the economic future of the EC/EU, I have had to temper this hope following a discussion with Pierre-André Buigues. He pointed out that our export performance in manufacturing within 'strong-demand/high-tech sectors' was relatively weak in comparison with our main competitors, the USA and Japan. Equally, with some national exceptions, the 'EC/EU had, over the period 1980–93, a weaker apparent labour productivity growth than its main competitors'. Fortunately, as a counterbalance to this unhappy state of affairs, he pointed out that over the same period 'the pattern of real incomes was growing more slowly than productivity'. Consequently, compared with our competitors, we have had a 'decline in real labour costs'. The message for the future is clear: we must release our creative and productive forces and embark forcefully on a policy of 'product differentiation'. Equally, we cannot afford to protect inefficient sectors of our economy while, at the same time, encouraging young people to seek refuge in social security.

THE FINAL WORDS

At this moment in time, we Europeans find ourselves facing many choices and dilemmas. The most important issues are:

(i)   Economically speaking, will Western Europe be competitive *vis-à-vis* the United States, Japan and South-East Asia?

(ii)   In this framework, will the EC Member States and the EFTA countries (where they are concerned) really make full and judicious use of the possible benefits which should emanate from the completion (hopefully by the end of this century) of the Single European Market (SEM)?

(iii)   How will the benefits emanating from (i) and (ii) be distributed among our citizens?

(iv)   Should we continue, as at present, along the road towards implementing a full economic and monetary union?

(v)   What kind of tranformation can best enable our national and Community institutions to serve us?

(vi)   How should we enlarge the European Community or Union? [16]

(vii) How should we best defend ourselves militarily?
(viii) What kind of Europe do we want?

My personal answer to these questions is that we want a free and democratic Europe where not only human rights are respected but where citizens are made fully aware of these rights.   At the economic level, we should aim at the optimum allocation of resources. To this end, our educational and training systems need to be judiciously reformed. In the political area, we need more open government at the Community level so that citizens can identify themselves with the EC or EU and the Council of Europe. Those countries which wish to integrate more deeply politically and in the economic and monetary fields should be allowed to do so. The others who prefer a looser form of union which will enable them to keep their cultural identities – and, after all, our diversity is our human, cultural and social wealth – should equally be allowed to do so. This is why, in this book, apart from welcoming the Single European Market – which the twelve EC Member States have accepted freely and without constraints – I would advocate the adoption of a policy of 'Europe à la carte'.

FOOTNOTE: THE UKRAINE AND START I

In November 1993, the Ukrainian Parliament finally ratified the START I Treaty. Unfortunately, it declared that the Treaty applied to only approximately half of the long-range nuclear warheads on its territory. Also, it disavowed Article 5 of the 1992 Lisbon Protocol whereby the Ukrainian Government had agreed to accede to the treaty to halt the spread of nuclear weapons – but as a non-nuclear state.

NOTES

1. P. Coffey, 1990, *Main Economic Policy Areas of the EC – Toward 1992*, Dordrecht: Kluwer Academic Publishers.
2. Anthony Lester, 1993, 'Britain Wrong on Human Rights', *Financial Times*, 26 May.
3. EC Commission, 1991, *The Development and the Future of the Common Agricultural Policy*, Brussels.

4. Alexis Jacquemin and David Wright, 1993, *The European Challenges Post-1992*, Edward Elgar, Aldershot.
5. In 1965, France, under President de Gaulle, practised a policy of the *chaise vide* – or empty chair – in Brussels. France returned when, the following year, the Luxemburg Compromise was adopted whereby an EC Member State, feeling that its vital national interests would be violated by a policy proposal, could use its right of veto in the Council of Ministers.
6. Peter Norman, 1993, 'EMU still firmly on Central bank agendas', *Financial Times*, 25 October.
7. Peter Norman, op. cit.
8. Commission of the European Communities, 1977, *Report of the Study Group on the Role of Public Finance in European Integration*, Brussels.
9. European Parliament, *A New Strategy for Social and Economic Cohesion after 1992*, Strasburg, 1991.
10. At that meeting, Romania was admitted as the 32nd member.
11. In October, 1993, the UK cancelled an air-launched missile project which France had hoped could be developed between the two countries. In contrast, however, Britain, France and Italy have agreed to build frigates together whilst the French and Germans are jointly constructing the Tiger anti-tank helicopter.
12. Currently, in the Yugoslavia-Bosnian conflict, the embargo control operation 'Sharp Guard', is a joint NATO/WEU operation.
13. Pierre-André Buigues, 1991, *L'Impact Sectoriel Du Marché Intérieur Sur L'Industrie*, European Commission, Brussels.
14. It should be noted that American companies, notably IBM, have long since treated the EC and EFTA as one internal market. This process has been intensified since the Community started to create the SEM.
15. Bureau Européen Des Unions des Consommateurs – sometimes known as the BEUC.
16. Throughout this work I have talked of the old European Economic Community (EEC) and, since February 1992, the European Community (EC). Of course, the European coal and steel community (ECSC) and Euratom still exist. At the political level, since the coming into force of the Treaty on European Union, at the beginning of November 1993, we also talk of European Union (EU).

Appendix 1: The Social Charter of the European Community

I. COMMUNITY CHARTER OF THE FUNDAMENTAL SOCIAL RIGHTS OF WORKERS

Whereas, under the terms of Article 117 of the EEC Treaty, the Member States have agreed on the need to promote improved living and working conditions for workers so as to make possible their harmonization while the improvement is being maintained;

Whereas following on from the conclusion of the European Councils of Hanover and Rhodes the European Council of Madrid considered that, in the context of the establishment of the single European market, the same importance must be attached to the social aspects as to the economic aspects and whereas, therefore, they must be developed in a balanced manner;

Whereas the completion of the internal market is the most effective means of creating employment and ensuring maximum well-being in the Community; whereas employment development and creation must be given first priority in the completion of the internal market, whereas it is for the Community to take up the challenges of the future with regard to economic competitiveness, taking into account, in particular, regional imbalances;

Whereas the social consensus contributes to the strengthening of the competitiveness of undertakings and of the economy as a whole and to the creation of employment; whereas in this respect it is an essential condition for ensuring sustained economic development;

Whereas the completion of the internal market must favour the approximation of improvements in living and working conditions, as well as economic and social cohesion with the European Community, while avoiding distortions of competition;

Whereas the completion of the internal market must offer improvements in the social field for workers of the European Community, especially in terms of freedom of movement, living and working conditions, health and safety at work, social protection, education and training;

Whereas, in order to ensure equal treatment, it is important to combat every form of discrimination, including discrimination on grounds of sex, colour, race, opinions and beliefs, and whereas, in a spirit of solidarity, it is important to combat social exclusion;

Whereas it is for Member States to guarantee that workers from non-member countries and members of their families who are legally resident in a Member State of the European Community are able to enjoy, as regards their living and working conditions, treatment comparable to that enjoyed by workers who are nationals of the Member State concerned;

Whereas inspiration should be drawn from the conventions of the International Labour Organization and from the European Social Charter of the Council of Europe;

Whereas the Treaty, as amended by the Single European Act, contains provisions laying down the powers of the Community relating, inter alia, to the freedom of movement of workers (Articles 7, 48-51), to the right of establishment (Articles 52-58), to the social field under the conditions laid down in Articles 117-112 – in particular as regards the improvement of health and safety in the working environment (Article 118a), the development of the dialogue between management and labour at the European level (Article 118b), equal pay for men and women for equal work (Article 119) – to the general principles for implementing a common vocational training policy (Article 128), to economic and social cohesion (Article 130a and 130e) and, more generally, to the approximation of legislation (Articles 100, 100a and 235); whereas the implementation of the Charter must not entail an extension of the Community's powers as defined by the Treaties;

Whereas the aim of the present Charter is on the one hand to consolidate the progress made in the social field, through action by the Member States, the two sides of industry and the Community;

Whereas its aim is on the other hand to declare solemnly that the implementation of the Single European Act must take full account of the social dimension of the Community and that it is necessary in this context to ensure at appropriate levels the development of the social rights of workers of the European Community, especially employed workers and self-employed persons;

Whereas, in accordance with the conclusions of the Madrid European Council, the respective roles of Community rules, national legislation and collective agreements must be clearly established;

Whereas, by virtue of the principle of subsidiarity, responsibility for the initiatives to be taken with regard to the implementation of these social rights lies with the Member States or their constituent parts, and, within the limits of its powers, the European Community; whereas such implementation may take the form of laws, collective agreements or existing practices at the various appropriate levels and whereas it requires in many spheres the active involvement of the two sides of industry;

Whereas the solemn proclamation of fundamental social rights at European Community level may not, when implemented, provide grounds for any retrogression compared with the situation currently existing in each Member State.

HAVE ADOPTED THE FOLLOWING DECLARATION CONSTITUTING THE 'COMMUNITY CHARTER OF THE FUNDAMENTAL SOCIAL RIGHTS OF WORKERS':

Title I— Fundamental Social Rights of Workers

Freedom of movement

1. Every worker of the European Community shall have the right to freedom of movement throughout the territory of the Community, subject to the restrictions justified on grounds of public order, public safety or public health.

2. The right to freedom of movement shall enable any worker to

engage in any occuptation or profession in the Community in accordance with the principles of equal treatment as regards access to employment, working conditions and social protection in the host country.

3.   The right of freedom of movement shall also imply: harmonization of conditions of residence in all Member States, particularly those concerning family reunification; elimination of obstacles arising from the non-recognition of diplomas or equivalent occupational qualifications; improvement of the living and working conditions of frontier workers.

Employment and remuneration

4.   Every individual shall be free to choose and engage in an occupation according to the regulations governing each occupation.

5.   All employment shall be fairly remunerated. To this effect, in accordance with arrangements applying in each country: workers shall be assured an equitable wage, i.e. a wage sufficient to enable them to have a decent standard of living; workers subject to terms of employment other than an open-ended full time contract shall receive an equitable reference wage; wages may be withheld, seized or transferred only in accordance with the provisions of national law; such provisions should entail measures enabling the worker concerned to continue to enjoy the necessary means of subsistence for himself and his family.

6.   Every individual must be able to have access to public placement services free of charge.

Improvement of living and working conditions

7.   The completion of the internal market must lead to an improvement in the living and working conditions of workers in the European Community. This process must result from an approximation of these conditions while the improvement is being maintained, as regards in particular the duration and organization of working time and forms of employment other than open-ended contracts, such as fixed-term contracts, part-time working, temporary work and seasonal work.

The improvement must cover, where necessary, the development of certain aspects of employment regulations such as procedure for collective redundancies and those regarding bankruptcies.

8.   Every worker of the European Community shall have a right to a weekly rest period and to annual paid leave, the duration of which must be harmonized in accordance with national practices while the improvement is being maintained.

9.   The conditions of employment of every worker of the European Community shall be stipulated in laws, in a collective agreement or in a contract of employment, according to arrangements applying in each country.

Social protection

According to the arrangement applying in each country:

10.   Every worker of the European Community shall have a right to adequate social protection and shall, whatever his status and whatever the size of the undertaking in which he is employed, enjoy an adequate level of social security benefits.

Persons who have been unable either to enter or re-enter the labour market and have no means of subsistence must be able to receive sufficient resources and social assistance in keeping with their particular situation.

Freedom of association

11.   Employers and workers of the European Community shall have the right of association in order to constitute professional organizations or trade unions of their choice for the defence of their economic and social interests.

Every employer and every worker shall have the freedom to join or not to join such organizations without any personal or occupational damage being thereby suffered by him.

12.   Employers or employer's organizations, on the one hand, and workers' organizations, on the other, shall have the right to negotiate and conclude collective agreements under the conditions laid down by national legislation and practice.

The dialogue between the two sides of industry at European level which must be developed, may, if the parties deem it desirable, result in contractual relations, in particular at inter-occupational and sectoral level.

13. The right to resort to collective action in the event of a conflict of interests shall include the right to strike, subject to the obligations arising under national regulations and collective agreements.

In order to facilitate the settlement of industrial disputes the establishment and utilization at the appropriate levels of conciliation, mediation and arbitration procedures should be encouraged in accordance with national practice.

14. The internal legal order of the Member States shall determine under which conditions and to what extent the rights provided for in Articles 11 to 13 apply to the armed forces, the police and the civil service.

Vocational training

15. Every worker of the European Community must be able to have access to vocational training and to receive such training throughout his working life. In the conditions governing access to such training there may be no discrimination on grounds of nationality.

The competent public authorities, undertakings or the two sides of industry each within their own sphere of competence, should set up continuing and permanent training systems enabling every person to undergo retraining more especially through leave for training purposes, to improve his skills or to acquire new skills, particularly in the light of technical developments.

Equal treatment for men and women

16. Equal treatment for men and women must be assured. Equal opportunities for men and women must be developed.

To this end, action should be intensified wherever necessary to ensure the implementation of the principle of equality between men and women as regards in particular access to employment, remuneration, working conditions, social protection, education, vocational training and career development.

Measures should also be developed enabling men and women to reconcile their occupational and family obligations.

Information, consultation and participation for workers
17.   Information, consultation and participation for workers must be developed along appropriate lines, taking account of the practices in force in various Member States

This shall apply especially in companies or groups of companies having establishments or companies in several Member States of the European Community.
18.   Such information, consultation and participation must be implemented in due time, particularly in the following cases:
–   when technological changes which, from the point of view of working conditions and work organization, have major implications for the work force are introduced into undertakings;
–   in connection with restructuring operations in undertakings or in cases of mergers having an impact on the employment of workers;
–   in cases of collective redundancy procedures;
–   when transfrontier workers in particular are affected by employment policies pursued by the undertaking where they are employed.

Health protection and safety at the workplace
19.   Every worker must enjoy satisfactory health and safety conditions in his working evironment. Appropriate measures must be taken in order to achieve further harmonization of conditions in this area while maintaining the improvements made.

These measures shall take account, in particular, of the need for the training, information, consultation and balanced participation of workers as regards the risks incurred and the steps taken to eliminate or reduce them.

The provisions regarding implementation of the internal market shall help to ensure such protection.

Protection of children and adolescents
20.   Without prejudice to such rules as may be favourable to young people, in particular those ensuring their preparation for work through vocational training, and subject to derogations limited to certain light work, the minimum employment age must not be lower than the minimum school-leaving age and, in any case, not lower than 15 years.

21. Young people who are in gainful employment must receive equitable remuneration in accordance with national practice.

22. Appropriate measures must be taken to adjust labour regulations applicable to young workers so that their specific needs regarding development, vocational training and access to employment are met,.

The duration of work must, in particular, be limited – and night work prohibited in the case of workers under eighteen years of age, save in the case of certain jobs laid down in national legislation or regulations.

23. Following the end of compulsory education, young people must be entitled to receive initial vocational training of a sufficient duration to enable them to adapt to the requirements of their future working life: for young workers, such training should take place during working hours.

Elderly persons

According to the arrangements applying in each country:

24. Every worker of the European Community must, at the time of retirement, be able to enjoy resources affording him or her a decent standard of living.

25. Every person who has reached retirement age but who is not entitled to a pension or who does not have other means of subsistence, must be entitled to sufficient resources and to medical and social assistance specifically suited to his needs.

Disabled persons

26. All disabled persons, whatever the origin and nature of their disablement, must be entitled to additional concrete measures aimed at improving their social and professional integration.

These measures must concern, in particular, according to the capacities of the beneficiaries, vocational training, ergonomics, accessibility, mobility, means of transport and housing.

Title II – Implementation of the Charter

27. It is more particularly the responsibility of the Member States, in

accordance with the national practices, notably through legislative measures or collective agreements, to guarantee the fundamental social rights in this Charter and to implement the social measures indispensable to the smooth operation of the internal market as part of a strategy of economic and social cohesion.

28.   The European Council invites the Commission to submit as soon as possible initiatives which fall within its powers, as provided for in the Treaties, with a view to the adoption of legal instruments for the effective implementation, as and when the internal market is completed, of those rights which come within the Community's area of competence.

29.   The Commission shall establish each year, during the last three months, a report on the application of the Charter by the Member States and by the European Community.

30.   The report of the Commisssion shall be forwarded to the European Council, the European Parliament and the Economic and Social Committee.

II.   Report from the Presidency to the European Council

After a long and constructive discussion, the Presidency notes that the procedure defined by the European Council in Madrid for drawing up the Charter of the fundamental social rights of workers has been observed.

On the basis of the Commission's draft, the social partners were consulted on 17 and 18 October, the European Parliament was informed on 17 October, and the Economic and Social Committee on 18 October.

The Community Charter of the fundamental social rights of workers must express the Member States' desire to harness together economic development and social progress in the Community, while complying with the principle of subsidiarity and, in general, remaining strictly within the powers of the Community authorities as defined by the Treaties.

The amendments submitted by the Member States have been taken into account and a Presidency draft drawn up.   It defines the fundamental social rights of European workers in 26 Articles.

The Presidency has taken note of the Council's agreement to forward the attached draft Charter with a view to a decision on adoption by the European Council.

The United Kingdom delegation, having objections to a number of Articles of the Charter, maintained its general reservation.

The Presidency has noted that, before the European Council meets, the Commission intends to submit an action programme on the practical implementation of the rights laid down in this Charter.

It invites the Commission in so doing to take into account the requests made by a number of delegations relating inter alia to the length of annual leave, pay for public holidays and sickness leave, protection of children and adolescents, the situation of pregnant women and mothers of small children, integration of the disabled into the ordinary working environment, health and safety at the workplace, vocational guidance, the mutual recognition of qualifications and temporary work.

In addition, the Presidency wants genuine equality of treatment to be applied to all workers, and to cover all forms of work, in particular work which offers no long-term security. It believes that, allowing for the differences in situation, any worker employed in another Member State in the context of subcontracting or the award of public works contracts should enjoy equal treatment with employees of the host country.

In connection with the priorities which the Council has set itself regarding employment and vocational training, it hopes that the project to set up a European Employment Survey Authority will be examined by the Council at its meeting on 30 November, along with the Community programme for the development of continuing training for employees in undertakings.

Lastly, it stresses the importance which it attaches to continuation of the dialogue between management and labour, particularly as regards the implementation of the principles laid down in the Charter.

Europe Documents No. 1579, 8 November 1989

Appendix 2: Opinion of the EC Commission on an Equitable Wage

THE COMMISSION OF THE EUROPEAN COMMUNITIES

Having regard to the Treaty establishing the European Economic Community, and in particular Article 118 thereof,

Having regard to the opinion of the Economic and Social Committee,

Having regard to the opinion of the European Parliament,

Whereas reinforcing social and economic cohesion within the Community requires respect fo the principles of equity and social justice;

Whereas the completion of the internal market will bring dynamism and employment opportunities and will assist the growth of the European economy; whereas this increase in riches should benefit all the inhabitants of the Community;

Whereas this development will enable the companies within the Community to establish a strong position with regard to those sectors of the Market which have a potential for high added value and for development;

Whereas the quality, performance and commitment of the European labour force are fundamental advantages in world competition;

Whereas the persistence of very low wage levels raises problems of equity and social cohesion, which could be harmful to the effectiveness of the economy in the long term;

Whereas the Community Charter on the Fundamental Social Rights of Workers, emphasized, in its point 5, the principle that all employment shall be fairly remunerated;

Whereas the Commission in its Action Programme relating to the implementation of the said Charter acknowledged that wage-setting is a matter for the Member States and the social partners; whereas the Commission recognized that it has a responsibility for asserting its views on an important problem for a significant proportion of the working population;

Whereas on 24 June 1992 the Council adopted Recommendation 92/441/EEC on common criteria concerning sufficient resources and social assistance in social protection systems; and whereas this opinion complements that Recommendation;

Whereas the report of an expert working party has shown that in spite of the mechanisms already in place the problem of low pay is an issue in all countries of the European Community;

Whereas it is recalled that with regard to pay Community Law prohibits discrimination on the grounds of sex or nationality,

HEREBY DELIVERS THE FOLLOWING OPINION:

1. The right, referred to in the Community Charter of the Fundamental Social Rights of Workers, of all workers to be assured of an equitable wage should be reaffirmed, with particular attention being paid to the more vulnerable members of the labour force; the concept of 'an equitable wage' means that all workers should receive a reward for work done which in the context of the society in which they live and work is fair and sufficient to enable them to have a decent standard of living.

2. While operational definitions can best be established at national, regional or sectoral levels, the right can best be assured as far as the Community level is concerned by complying with the following prinicples:

the Community's future in the world economy lies in achieving high productivity and high quality employment. This objective should be pursued throughout the Community not only by increasing the rate of investment in capital equipment, but also by increasing investment in education and training, particularly in order to meet the

developing needs for qualifications on the part of companies and
workers and by the promotion of good industrial relations,
the pursuit of equitable wages is to be seen as part of the process of
achieving the Community's basic objectives of greater economic and
social cohesion and a more harmonious development within the
framework of an increasingly integrated European economy,
wages are determined as much by social as by economic factors.
While adjustments in wages may reflect structural changes on
demand and supply in industries, regions and skills, the increasingly
integrated Community labour market may well affect the social
preferences which influence national wage hierarchies.   The
Community should therefore seek ways of eliminating discriminatory
wage practices, as part of its wider social and economic objectives,
attitudes to traditionally low-paid groups should be reassessed.
Discrimination should be combated and equall opportunities
promoted in a variety of ways, including legislation, taxation and
administrative arrangements or consensus or collective bargaining.

3. To this end Member States should:
give substance to their commitment given in the Social Charter to
assure the right of all workers to an equitable wage, irrespective of
gender, disability, race, religion, ethnic origin or nationality,

take account of the principles outlined in point 2 in the development
of their economic and social policies,

take the following action to implement these principles:

**Action to improve labour market transparency with regard to
wages**
Action is needed at all levels to improve the labour market, in particular:

by improving transparency of the labour market by a better
collection and dissemination of comparable statistical information
about wage structures at Community, national and local levels to
enable more effective policies to be developed and thus remove

some of the causes of unfairness;
employment services have an important role in this respect,
by disseminating widely existing information about equitable reference wages.

Action designed to ensure that the right to an equitable wage is respected
Member States should take appropriate measures to ensure that the right to an equitable wage is protected, in particular by a reassessment of the adequacy of existing arrangements to protect the right to an equitable wage, including consideration of the following:

further legislation including legislation on discrimination, in particular on grounds of gender, race, ethnic origin or religion,
means of ensuring fair treatment of workers in all age groups and for homeworkers,
mechanisms for the establisment of negotiated minima and the strengthening of collective bargaining arrangements.

These arrangements could be supplemented by:

development of codes of good practice with regard to the treatment of weaker groups of workers on the labour market who are susceptible to low wages,
improved arrangements for providing information about the labour market, particularly with regard to rates of pay, while avoiding imposing undue burdens on small and medium-sized undertakings,
provision of information about discriminatory practices.

The Member States should ensure that the measures taken do not force low-paid workers into the informal economy and do not encourage recourse to unlawful employment practices.
The Member States should also ensure that the measures do not have a negative impact on job creation.
They should take the necessary measures to ensure that the wages agreed in contractual labour relationships are effectively and fully paid

and that employees are correctly paid in respect of periods of leave or sickness.

Action in favour of human resource development
Member States should take the necessary measures to improve the long-term productivity and earnings potential of the workforce. These measures should include a major effort to increase investment in human resources at all levels and all stages of development, including secondary and tertiary education, initial training, retraining, continuous training and individual development.

4. The social partners are invited to:

> address all the issues raised by this opinion at Community, national, regional and local level, in particular to examine what contribution they can make to ensuring the right of every worker to an equitable wage.

5. For its part the Commission considers that it is pertinent:

> to take appropriate measures to improve the quality of information available at Community level, in particular with regard to wage structures. To this end the Commission proposes to undertake a new, revised, Survey on the Structure of Earnings in order to provide more rapid information and to adopt existing statistical tools. The information so collected will be widely disseminated and can provide a basis for discussion at national and Community levels,
> to contribute towards a better matching of vocational training arrangements to the developing needs for qualifications and retraining of both workers and businesses, by ensuring the collection and dissemination of experience in this area and encouraging co-operation between those concerned,
> to encourage the development of exchanges across the Community on the practices within firms with regard to remuneration,
> to undertake further studies, in collaboration with the Member States and the social partners, to seek to promote a convergence of equitable wage policies within the Member States.

6. The Commission will submit a report to the Council, the Economic and Social Committee and the European Parliament, after consultation with the social partners, within three years after the adoption of this opinion on the basis of information which will be requested from the Member States on the progress made and the obstacles encountered. Thereafter, progress will be monitored every two years.

Official Journal of the European Communities, 11 September 1993

Appendix 3: Joint EEC–EFTA Statement on the State of the Negotiations over the European Economic Area (EEA)

On May 13, 1991, the Ministers from the EEC and EFTA countries managed to overcome numerous difficulties to adopt a 'joint statement' on negotiations over the European Economic Area (EEA), reaffirming the political will to arrive at an agreement. This statement does not solve all the difficulties; in certain cases it simply invites the negotiators to look for solutions. However, it does represent the fundamental political document for the decisive state of these difficult negotiations.

We reproduce here the text in full:

MINISTERIAL MEETING BETWEEN THE EUROPEAN COMMUNITY, ITS MEMBER STATES AND THE COUNTRIES OF THE EUROPEAN FREE TRADE ASSOCIATION: JOINT DECLARATION

1. The Ministers of the Member States and the Commission of the European Communities and the Ministers of the Member States of the European Free Trade Association and Liechtenstein met in Brussels on 13 May 1991.
2. The meeting was chaired, for the Community, by Mr. Jacques Poos, Minister of Foreign Affairs of Luxemburg, President–in–Office of the Council of the European Communities, and for the EFTA countries by Mr. Wolfgang Schussel, Minister for Economic Affairs of Austria, Chairman of the EFTA Council. The Commission of the European

Communities was represented by Mr. Frans Andriessen, Vice-President. The list of participating Minsisters is attached. Mr Georg Reisch, Secretary–General of EFTA, also participated in the meeting.

3. Ministers confirmed their commitment to conclude, before the summer, negotiations on a comprehensive EEA agreement, based on equality which should ensure the greatest possible mutual interest for the parties concerned as well as the global and balanced character of their co-operation.

4. On the basis of the respective oral reports on the current state of the negotiations, they took note with satisfaction of the considerable progress achieved in the negotiations since their last joint meeting in December 1990.

5. They noted that agreement had been achieved on several important elements of the EEA agreement and concluded that solutions now seemed possible on the remaining open issues. Recalling that final agreement was dependent on a mutually acceptable solution to all questions covered by the negotiations, both substantive and institutional, as well an overall balance of benefits, rights and obligations, they encouraged negotiators to pursue their work actively in order to find solutions to the outstanding problems.

6. With reference to the issues mentioned in their Joint Declaration of 19 December 1990 they noted the following developments.

7. They welcomed progress achieved in the definition of solutions required for the operation of a system ensuring equal conditions of competition including state aids throughout the EEA. They noted convergence on the main elements defining the respective role of, and the co-operation between the EC Commission and the independent EFTA structure (with equivalent powers and similar functions as those exercised by the EC Commission). They encouraged negotiators to finalize the negotiations as rapidly as possible, including on more detailed criteria for the attribution of cases between the two sides and on the role of the judicial mechanism.

8. The participants welcomed the pragmatic solutions agreed upon reconciling a high level of protection in the field of health, safety and the environment with the free circulation of goods. This will ensure that most of the relevant Community *acquis* will be applied in full by

the EFTA countries as from 1 January 1993. In some other areas, free circulation within the EEA will be guaranteed from 1 January 1993 on the basis of Community *acquis* although EFTA countries' national legislations may be maintained during a transitional period. In relation to motor vehicles agreement was reached on free circulation as of 1 January 1995 on the basis of the Community *acquis*. EFTA countries may however maintain national legislation until new Community rules are introduced which will be dealt with according to procedures laid down in the Agreement. For certain products (i.e. fertilizers containing cadmium, CFCs, Halons) an open-ended transitional period has been agreed subject to a review in 1995.

Sectors where solutions have to be found before the end of negotiations are now reduced to those of dangerous substances, chemical substances/preparations and pesticides. Negotiators have been encouraged to pursue their work on these issues.

9. As regards other questions related to goods, the participants noted good progress on public procurement, product liability, testing and certification and EC mark, and intellectual property. The agreement will contain a number of elements increasing co-operation in customs matters and improving and simplifying rules of origin. Further improvements will be sought in the framework of the Agreement.

10. Moreover progress was noted on steel which both sides agree to bring under the coverage of the EEA Agreement in as far as the provisions of the bilateral Free Trade Agreements for ECSC products, which will be maintained, do not apply. Further progress has been achieved in the area of energy where agreement has been reached on the inclusion of part of the EC *acquis*. More work is necessary on the *acquis* with provisions relating to difficulties of supply.

11. They also welcomed the agreement in the areas related to the free movement of capital and services. The relevant Community *acquis* will be introduced by the EFTA countries from 1 January 1993 with the exception of some elements for which transitional periods will apply. Moreover in the area of capital movements the EFTA countries concerned will apply their present legislation in a liberal manner during the transitional period. Further work is necessary concerning the EC Broadcasting Directive. Furthermore they welcomed the agreement

reachedon the outline of economic and monetary co-operation.

12. They noted further progress in the transport area, a key factor in the EEA context in relation to the free movement both of goods and services. They concluded that a comprehensive solution in transport has to be found. They urged negotiators shortly to conclude the ongoing bilateral transit negotiations taking into account the specific interests of some EEA peripheral countries.

13. Further work remains to be done in the area of free movement of persons.

14. They noted that agreement had been reached that in a number of horizontal areas where EC *acquis* will be taken over by the EFTA countries (company law, social policy and environmental policy) transitional periods up to two years in general will apply.

They welcomed the agreement reached to strengthen and broaden co-operation outside the four freedoms (flanking policies) in the framework of the Community's activities in the area such as research and development including information services, environment, education, training and youth, social policy, consumer protection, small and medium-sized enterprises, tourism and audiovisual sector, insofar as these matters are not regulated by other titles of the Agreement. They noted that there are now a substantial convergence of views as regards the elements which should figure in the EEA Agreement to provide a firm legal basis for a comprehensive and dynamic co-operation.

They encouraged negotiators to press ahead with their work on the few remaining questions on which agreement still has to be reached.

15. The participants took note of the progress in the agricultural area. They confirmed their determination to achieve within the EEA a higher degree of liberalization of agricultural trade in the framework of their respective agricultural policies. An evolutionary clause will be included in the EEA Agreement. Moreover, EFTA countries will abolish or reduce import duties from 1 January 1993 on a range of products of a particular importance to the less developed regions of the Community. Particular attention will also be paid to the objective of abolishing trade barriers resulting from veterinary and phytosanitary regulations. In the latter areas the EFTA countries will take over, to the maximum extent possible, the EC *aquis*. Moreover, concrete measures will be introduced form 1 January 1993 in the form of reciprocal

The Future of Europe

bilateral agreements between the EC and the EFTA countries under the umbrella of the EEA Agreement.

Finally, trading conditions will be facilitated for processed agricultural products. They agreed that negotiations on all these issues should now be actively pursued and finalized as quickly as possible, given the importance of the agricultural sector as an element of balance in the Agreement as well as in the context of the reduction of regional social and economic disparities.

16. Recalling that they attached the same importance to the inclusion of fisheries into the EEA Agreement, they determined the need for urgent and increased negotiating effort, in order to arrive at a solution combining satisfactorily the interests of both sides before the end of the negotiations.

With regard to fisheries, the ministers specifically refer to §4 of this Declaration, stating that the final agreement was dependent on a mutually acceptable solution to all questions covered by the negotiations: there must, at the end, be an overall balance of benefits, rights and obligations for each Contracting Party.

17. Urgent further work was also required with regard to the ways and means of attaining the important objective of reducing regional economic and social disparities. This objective is essential to ensure a satisfactory balance of the EEA Agreement. They took note of the request of the Community and of the readiness of the EFTA countries to consider the creation of a financial mechanism through which appropriate efforts will be made to the attainment of this objective. Concrete modalities should now be worked out.

18. As regards legal and institutional questions the participants reaffirmed the principles set out in the Joint Declaration of 19 December 1990. They considered that operational institutional solutions should be arrived at in order to achieve maximum legal homogeneity within the European Economic Area without compromising decision-making autonomy of the Contracting Parties, the process of integration of the European Communities and the specific nature of Community law. With this in mind, they treated in particular the following points:

19. They agreed on the need to provide in the agreement for a general safeguard clause which could be triggered into action whenever

serious economic, societal, and/or environmental difficulties of a sectoral or regional nature were arising. The Contracting Parties could, in unilateral declarations noted by the Diplomatic Conference, make any specific points they wished on the possible application of the general clause. They also confirmed the points in this connection made in the Joint Declaration of 19 December 1990.

20. They also stressed the importance, in order to ensure maximum legal homogeneity, of developing, as regards questions concerning the European Economic Area, an ongoing process of information and consultation in the course of the Community legislative process and likewise of involving experts from the EFTA countries as widely as possible according to the areas concerned in the preparatory stage of draft measures to be submitted subsequently to the Committees by the Commission. In this regard, they noted that when drawing up its proposals the Commission would refer to experts from the EFTA countries on the same basis as those from the Member States. Further, they noted that pragmatic solutions for certain specific problems could be discussed and the the status of the EFTA countries in the Committees relating to the flanking policies would take full account of their possible financial participation in the projects concerned.

20. Recalling that decisions at European Economic Area level are taken on a consensus basis by the Community on one side and the EFTA countries speaking with one voice on the other side, they recognized that should a serious and important difficulty arise in those areas which in the EFTA countries came within the competence of the legislator, this difficulty should be subjected to examination by the Joint Committee, which would try first of all to seek a mutually acceptable solution which would allow to maintain the Agreement in its entirety without prejudice to the possibility of invoking subsequently, where necessary, the general safeguard clause and proportionate rebalancing measures.

22. The participants stressed the need to have in the European Economic Area an effective system of surveillance composed on the one hand of the Commission and on the other of an EFTA mechanism working in similar way and also an independent judicial mechanism.

23. As regards the independent judicial mechanism, the following

principles will be taken into account:

A. Nomination of seven judges from the EFTA countries;
B. Creation of an independent EEA Court composed of five judges, functionally integrated with the EC Court of Justice and which would be competent to give rulings:

concerning dispute settlement (including when necessary interpretation of the EEA rules) on request of the Joint Body or the Contracting Parties,

concerning disputes between the EFTA Surveillance Body and an EFTA country,

concerning cases brought by enterprises or States against decisions of the EFTA structure in the field of competition (including State aid).

C. Reinforcement of the legal homogeneity within the EEA through opening of intervention possibilities for EFTA countries before the EC Court of Justice and through a procedure inspired by that of the Lugano Convention.

24. They noted that the EFTA Member States were prepared to introduce provisions in their internal legislation to the effect that rules of the Agreement establishing an European Economic Area shall prevail in cases of possible conflicts between these rules and other provisions of their internal legal order.

Europe Documents No. 1712, 22 May 1991

Appendix 4: Current Membership of the Western European Union (WEU)

At the time of writing, the Western European Union (WEU) consists of ten full members, i.e. Belgium, France, Germany, Greece (membership not ratified), Italy, Luxemburg, the Netherlands, Portugal, Spain and the United Kingdom.

There are also three associate members, Iceland, Norway and Turkey, and two observer members, Denmark and Ireland. Furthermore, the so-called Consultation Forum includes nine countries from Central and Eastern Europe, i.e. Bulgaria, the Czech Republic, Estonia, Hungary, Latvia, Lithuania, Poland, Romania and Slovakia.

Appendix 5: Freezing of the Composition of the ECU

In accordance with the coming into force, on 1 November 1993, of the Treaty on European Union, the composition of the currency basket making up the European Currency Unit (ECU) was 'frozen'. Thus, this composition of the ECU is henceforth that of 28 October 1993, which is shown below.

COMPOSITION OF THE ECU ON 28 OCTOBER 1993

		Amounts in National Currencies	Weights
DM	(Germany)	0.6242	32.63
FF	(France)	1.332	19.89
DG	(Netherlands)	0.2198	10.23
BEF	(Belgium)	3.431	8.28
DKR	(Denmark)	0.1976	2.56
IRP	(Ireland)	0.008552	1.06
Sub-total 1			**74.66**
ITL	(Italy)	151.8	8.18
UKP	(United Kingdom)	0.08784	11.45
DRA	(Greece)	1.44	0.53
PTA	(Spain)	6.885	4.50
ESC	(Portugal)	1.393	0.71
Sub-total 2			**25.34**
TOTAL			100.00

Appendix 6: Commission to hold Exchange of Views on Institutional Adjustments linked to Accession of EFTA Countries – Descriptive Document by Council Presidency

BRUSSELS, 17/10/1993 (AGENCE EUROPE) – On Wednesday, the European Commission is expected to hold an exchange of views on institutional adjustments in the Community linked to accession by Austria, Sweden, Norway and Finland. The following elements make up the backdrop of this discussion:

- as decided by the Heads of Government at the Lisbon Summit, *the accession of EFTA countries should be achieved without major institutional changes*. The in-depth discussion on Community institutions and their functioning with a view to reform will take place at the intergovernmental conference planned, in principle, for 1996 (and which could, according to some, be brought forward);
- the institutional modifications made necessary by this first enlargement are those which *result from the insertion of new member States into the institutions, in principle without modifying the way the institutions work.*

As real reform on the insitutions is to be ruled out at this stage, the *current general principles* remain valid, in particular the following:

a) every Member State is represented in every institution. This is the principle followed on the occasion of previous enlargements;

b) the relative position of each Member State is fixed essentially according to demographic criteria. Member States have therefore been placed in different groups according to population size (nevertheless, certain political factors have also been taken into consideration).

The Council Presidency has, in the meanwhile, established a 'note' *which in no way constitutes a proposal* by the Presidency but which is simply a description of the current situation and the situation that would result from applying the criteria applied until now to the enlarged Community. The results of this neutral and descriptive document are:

1. *European Parliament.* The Parliament itself has requested, by its resolutions of 10 June 1992 and 15 July 1993, that the following seats be granted to the four applicant States: *Sweden 21, Austria 20, Finland 16, Norway 15.*
The total number of MEPs would thus increase to 639 (the current repartition being: Germany 99, France, United Kingdom and Italy 87 each; Spain 64; Netherlands 31; Belgium, Greece and Portugal 25 each; Denmark 16; Ireland 15; Luxemburg 6).

2. *Council.* Each Member State has a seat at the Council, but with different voting weight in *majority votes*. By applying the the current criteria to the enlarged EC, the situation would become the following:

Member State	Population (in millions on 1/1/1993)	Votes
Germany	80.6	10
France	57.5	10
Italy	56.9	10
United Kingdom	57.9	10
Spain	39.1	8
Belgium	10.0	5
Greece	10.3	5
Netherlands	15.2	5
Portugal	9.8	5

Austria	7.9	4 or 5
Sweden	8.6	4 or 5
Denmark	5.2	3
Ireland	3.5	3
Norway	4.3	3
Finland	5.0	3
Luxembourg	0.4	2
Total		90 - 92

Qualified majority is currently 54 out of 76, which means that voting can be *blocked by a minority* of 23 votes. By bringing the number of votes up to 90 (or 92), keeping the same proportions, the qualified majority would become:

- 64 votes out of 90 if Austria and Sweden have 5 votes each, the blocking minority remaining 27 votes;
- 66 votes out of 92 if Austria and Sweden have 5 votes each, the blocking minority remaining 27 votes.

The alphabetical order for *rotating presidency* (in national languages) would be: Norway and Austria after the Netherlands; Finland and Sweden after Portugal.

3. *Commission.* As a commissioner of the nationality of each new Member State must be nominated, the *number of European commissioners would increase from 17 to 21.*

4. *Court of Justice.* All twelve Member States currently have a judge. The thirteenth judge (an equal number being necessary for Plenum deliberations) is, by rotation, of the nationality of one of the following Member States: Germany, France, Italy, United Kingdom and Spain. On the other hand, there are 6 advocate general (including four of German, French, Italian and British nationality and the others of another nationality, in turn).

With the four new accessions, there would be seventeen judges and eight advocate generals, without modifications of the current criteria.

5. *Court of Auditors.* The number of members would be increased

from 12 to 16, one per country.

6. *Economic and Social Committee.* The number of advisors would increase from 189 to 229 (or to 231) by attributing 11 (or 12) members to Austria and Sweden, 9 to Norway and 9 to Finland.

7. *Committee of the Regions.* The situation is identical to that described for the Economic and Social Committee.

The Presidency's descriptive document does not cover the European Investment Bank (EIB) or the ECSC Advisory Committee.

Europe Documents No. 6088 pp 5-6, 18 October 1993

Index